s?

Carlene
Kelsey

SANTA'S DIARIES

Santa's Diaries

A Year of Mayhem, Merriment, and Miracles at the North Pole

Nicholas F. Christmas

DELIVERED BY
J.M. & V.C. Tannenbaum

Library of Congress Cataloging-in-
Publication Data is available on file.

ISBN 978-1-59921-802-1

This book was conceived, designed,
and produced by
Ivy Press
210 High street, Lewes
East Sussex, BN7 2NS, U.K.
www.ivy-group.co.uk

Printed in China

10 9 8 7 6 5 4 3 2 1

Creative Director: Peter Bridgewater
Publisher: Jason Hook
Editorial Director: Tom Kitch
Art Director: Wayne Blades
Senior Project Editor: Polita Caaveiro
Designer: Clare Barber
Illustrator: Neil Gower
Additional graphics: Luna Creative
Concept: Viv Croot, Jane Moseley

PICTURE CREDITS
Bridgeman Art Library: p68 (br), p126;
Corbis: p84, p93 (l), p130, p140 (bl), p141;
Superstock photos: p66 (tl);
Topfoto: p4, p147.

PERSONAL DETAILS

Name: Nicholas F. Christmas, aka Santa Claus

Home address: Yule Lodge, Snowman's Lane, Lapland, North Pole, NP 2412

Home telephone: secret

Work address: Santacorp, North Pole, NP 2412

Work telephone: 00 01 2412 000

E-mail: huh?

In case of accident please notify: Mrs. Sugarplum Christmas (Mamma C.), Yule Lodge, North Pole

Birthsign: Cancer (June 25)

Blood group: Ho positive

Doctor: Doc. Saylittle

Dentist: Doc. Toof

Life coach: Guru Nagaratha Wang O'Shaunessy

Allergies: green vegetables

ESSENTIAL INFORMATION:

Favorite color: red

Suit size: roomy

Boot size: comfy

Favorite foods: cookies, cupcakes, cheesecake, muffins, stollen, strudel, pizza, pie, chocolate, candies, gingerbread, ice cream, marshmallows, whip cream

Clubs and associations: Sleigh Slim (lifetime member); Union of Finishing, Glazing and Varnishing Craftsmen

Hobbies: football & baseball (spectator); travel; vacations; giving presents; partying; eating

If found please return immediately to the above address for a substantial or edible reward.

ƖNTRODUCTION

You have in your hands, dear reader, a very special diary. The thoughts, musings, and memorabilia it contains are unique. It covers just one year in the long and colorful life of one Nicholas Christmas, better known to us all as Santa Claus. We feel honored, indeed privileged, to bring to the world such an exciting book by someone of whom we are all so fond. Santa means so much to all of us, but after reading his diary, we are sure he will mean so much more.

When we first approached Santa via his P.A., Byron Poindexter, it was because we felt that our international expertise and years of experience at raising brand awareness could enhance Santa's unique profile, so that his presence was felt, however subliminally, throughout the year. We did not want Santa to be just for Christmas. We wanted him to be in our hearts and minds 365 days a year, 24/7. We are all aware of who he is and what he does, but how many of us really know Santa? We know what he does on Christmas Day—or C-Day as he refers to it in the diary— but not how he spends the rest of his year. We do not know what makes Santa tick, what jingles his bells. We do not know his hopes and fears, his ups and downs, his challenges and triumphs, his loves and hates, his home life with Mamma C., or what he eats for breakfast. In fact he was a red-coated enigma until we, Team Tannenbaum, persuaded him to allow us to publish his own personal record, his very own, very personal, diary.

However, when we looked at the first draft of the edited diary, we realized that it only told half the story. After a few throw-it-against-the-wall-and-see-if-it-sticks sessions, and some inter-team full and frank discussion, we came to the conclusion that we would be cheating Santa's worldwide fanbase if we didn't show our own workings on the project as well as Santa's true and unedited thoughts as he felt them, written down in ink on the page. In consultation with our now ex-editor, we decided to interpolate the notes and comments we made at the time—to physically insert them into the diary—so that the whole story could be told. At that point, we also realized we didn't need an editor. A few readers may wonder why we have included some material that other people have suggested might show us—and possibly even Santa—in a bad light; but we believe that there is no such thing as a bad light, just bad lighting design; we also feel that this is the 21st century and a postmodern approach is the only way to spin a revitalizing leftfield twist on a much-loved brand, which is solidly established but maybe a little tired.

As you come to know Santa through his diary, you will find a complex, caring being, both a team player and a leader. He has slow days and bad days, fast days and good days, mood swings and many happy moments—in fact he occasionally comes across as a tad bipolar—but this is only to be expected of someone who, by the nature of his existence as an anthropomorphic representation conjured up by the whole of humanity, must be in touch with his more sensitive feminine side as well as his robust, red-suited masculinity.

He is Supersanta. He is Santastic. His diary is a page turner. Read on.

Team Tannenbaum

SUNRISE—CHRISTMAS DAY
Perfect Sleighdown!

C-DAY DEBRIEFING
SUNRISE +1

Mamma C. suggested that I log my first thoughts while they are still fresh (and before I go to sleep and forget everything!). Main points:

🌲 Santa Transport Vehicle (STV) performed admirably, although we did lose one bell on re-entry and had slight friction burn when banking to starboard—maybe those ceramic runner shields just aren't up to the job! Any way we can avoid those near misses we keep having with Père Noël?

🌲 Clear night, bright stars, infinite visibility, aside from foggy Seattle patch.

🌲 Santanav wobble over Bermuda Triangle meant that we had to make two circuits, but time was made up over Pacific on way to Australia when we switched to Rudolph Overdrive.

🌲 Naughty or Nice list ran almost without a hitch, though we may get a complaint in from Idaho—maybe we need to update the system...

🌲 Chimney compliance much better this year, but soot goggles might be the way forward to avoid eye burn.

What a sight!

SUNRISE + 4

Much mellower after a mug or three of hot chocolate and a few cinnamon and raisin cupcakes (no diet on C-Day). It was a great trip, like it always is; once me and the deer

are up and running, and the stars are whizzing by, all the worries melt away and I am in the zone. Could have done without that near miss with Père Noël over Montreal, but only a bit of a dent at the rear, so no sweat. Thank goodness for the constant snacks—help to keep out the cold. A few cookies and I'm back up the chimney in no time! Will write more later—first must eat!

SUNRISE + 6

Just about to join the workforce for our grand C-Day Banquet. Fourteen courses, all chosen by me! Mamma C. excelled herself with her red and gold themed Christmas tree and we're all going to exchange presents. I'm giving everybody hand-made earmuffs. I hope they'll be pleased.

Santacorp
Grand Christmas Works Lunch

House Cocktail —The Santacorp Sleigher

Quail egg mini omelets,
Smoked salmon blinis,
Turnip and mangel wurzel pastry parcels
Lemming kebabs

Soup with hot rolls and / or oat mash dumplings
Poached salmon on a bed of pine needles
Broiled goose stuffed with a chicken stuffed
with a grouse stuffed with a lark
Served with potatoes, red onion marmalade,
chestnut purée and green pea tartlets
Carrot soufflé with bran mash royale

Holly and ivy sorbet
Cheeseboard

SUNSET + 4

Our fantastic lunch turned into a great impromptu party; everybody letting their hair down after all that hard work—elves, deer, even Stiltskin. Mamma C. was still cutting a mean rug when I snuck down to the stables to say goodnight to the team. Now off for a long soak in the bath.

DECEMBER 26

Phew. Still a bit dazed from the banquet—Mamma C. says it was 'turkey overload' but this morning feels like the first time I've been able to take a breath. Still, mission accomplished. All safely back at North Pole base camp.
The trusty Santacorp team delivered the goods again. Millions of them and to all the well-behaved children around the world; on time, right present in right stocking—although we'll see what Personnel has to say about that later. I don't think I was spotted—apart from the usual cats and dogs. Had a close shave in Miami when I slipped on some marble and landed head first into a plate full of triple-choco donuts—felt dizzy so sat down and polished them off. For some reason the chimney seemed smaller on the way up!

check out my new soot goggles!

This year's snacks: the good, and the not-so-good

9 out of 10!

Hmmm... not so sure

Got a great book on ice
sculpting from Frosty the
Snowman this year with
this cute gift tag to
match. And Rudolph
gave me an awesome
Polaroid camera!

Totally exhausted but
made calls to a few of
the European franchises;
spoke to Père Noël,
Babbo Natale and D.E.R.
Weihnachtsmann.
They all made sleigh-
down safely and no
reports of Glimpsing or
Wrong Toy Events, so Go Team!

to Santa
from Frosty
xx

Looking forward to some rest and relaxation, but Mamma C.
has just handed me an article about a new fitness regime for
men of a certain age. Plus, there was a book in my stocking
and it certainly isn't the photography manual I was hoping
for—or one of my usual chill-out thrillers. More 'Diet Detox'
than 'Daggers at Dawn.' The Santa suit felt distinctly
looser this year but Mamma C. says it's only due to 'fabric
fatigue'... I know how it feels.

Check if
    anybody saw me...

Ask Stiltskin
for delivery stats.

SLEEP

SLEEP

ZZZZ

SLEEP

SLEEP

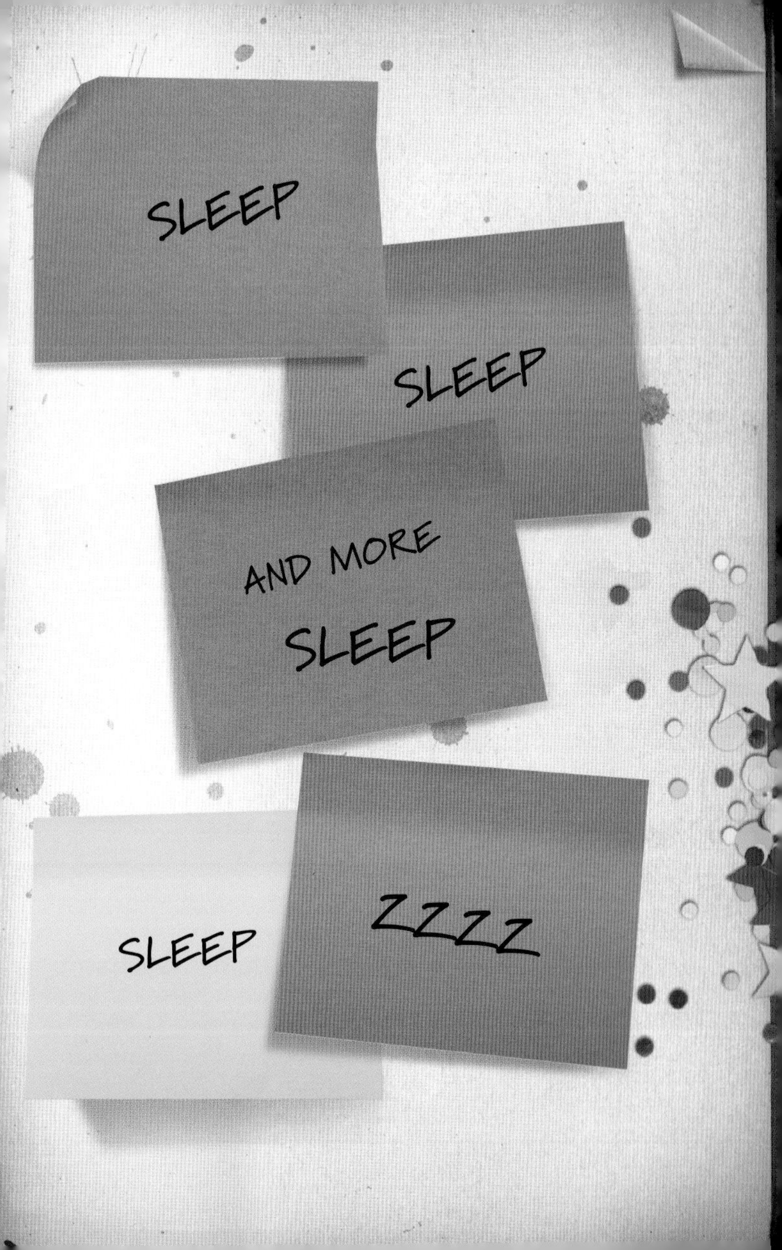
SLEEP
SLEEP
AND MORE
SLEEP
SLEEP
ZZZZ

DECEMBER 29

Dreamt it was Christmas Eve already and I was trying on my Santa suit. It was way too tight round the middle and the pants split when I tried to move. All the elves were laughing at me, and even Rudolph was holding back a chuckle. I woke in a terrible panic at 3:00am and Mamma C. brought me a mug of hot milk. She told me it was a classic anxiety dream and we should do some 'prioritizing' first thing in the morning. I wasn't sure that would help—I have enough priorities!—but kept that one to myself. Moved to the den so she could get some sleep. Began some lists but gave up again. Succumbed to my secret cookie stash and slept like a baby.

DECEMBER 30

Spent some time today reflecting on my achievements last year, and what I can do to improve things in the coming months. Tried not to think about the mishaps—Mamma C. says that's 'wasted energy.' But there is so much to think about. Have I disappointed anyone?—given a present to someone naughty?, forgotten someone nice? Did any kids wake up? Every street corner seemed to have a security camera, not to mention all those families trying to sneak a peek... What will be this year's must-have toy? Am I just getting too old? Is it just me, or are the chimneys smaller these days? Ate six cookies in one hit. Felt worse. Ate more cookies to stave off the sugar low.

TO DO LIST

- Thank-you cards to Easter Bunny, Tooth Fairy and Frosty
- Find new PA
- Sleep!
- Take suit to cleaners
- Beard maintenance
- Check on Abominable Snowman— haven't seen him lately...
- Fill snack cupboards—low on Triple Dunkeeos and Saltee-vees
- Have a look at those last-minute 'nice' appeals for next year

Crumble
Chocolate
Chip
Cookies

® Dunkers

My first Polaroid! I'm quite good at this!

Replenish cookie tins in den, sleigh, workshop, office, garage, and games room.

DECEMBER 31

Tried to get into the factory last night to try out a few prototypes for next year without anyone interfering—the 'Go-Lo Vibro Exercise Plate' sounds downright scary. I think I need to keep more of an eye on Santa Off Shoots Inc. this year. The building was locked up and Mamma C. had hidden the key somewhere. Must have burnt off a few cals just getting there and back without being spotted...

Vibro-tastic!

JANUARY 1

Happy New Year! Mamma C. and I stepped out for a beautiful New Year's Eve stroll at precisely midnight—and were treated to nature's own fireworks—the Northern Lights in all their glory. What a sight!

It's better up North!

JANUARY 2

Maintenance unit rang to ask if gifts had been particularly heavy this year, as there seemed to be more 'drag and wear' to the axles, whatever that means. Spoke to Rudolph who confirmed that the load felt bigger than usual. Suspect the bill will be too. I notice he said 'load' and not 'gifts'— and he raised an eyebrow at me. Rudolph sounded tired and rather cross. Not like him. I suppose we've all had long days though. Maybe I need to loosen the reins.

277989

Snowhite
LAUNDRY AND DRYCLEAN COMPANY

367973

$500 SANTA'S SUIT

NAME: N. Christmas
ADDRESS: Yule Lodge

RECEIPT

1	MENS :	
2	(SUITS)	$50
3	PANTS	
4	COATS	
5	(BELTS)	$5
6	JACKETS	
7	SHIRTS	
8	LADIES:	
9	DRESSES	
10	BLOUSES	
11	SWEATERS	
12	Additional repairs to pants	$445
	Total pieces: 2 Total price:	$500

JANUARY 3

Woke bright and early after yesterday's rest. Mamma C. brought me a wonderful cup of tea (accompanied not by cookies I noticed, but one of her looks) and chatted to me while I had a reviving pine needle bubble bath. Apparently the No.1 Santa suit is at the dry cleaners as usual, but will be there for longer due to the need for serious 'posterior' repairs. Felt anxious again. Dreams do often come true but not always in a good way.

What's eating Rudolph?

Try to find out.

JANUARY 4

Sent Santa sack to Technical Department for post-Christmas maintenance. Mr. Grimsby's eye started twitching when he saw the condition it was in, and now he's sent this memo. Don't they realize it's been around the world? Mamma C. is insisting I do a weigh-in on January 5. Dreading it. I know I won't sleep well tonight.

977989

LAPLAND MOTORS

CUSTOMER ORDER NO 1212   2 Jan

NAME Mr. S. Claus

ADDRESS Yule Lodge

Lapland

AMOUNT QUANTITY		DESCRIPTION	PRICE	
1	2x	new sleigh runners	@$50	$100
2	1x	replace wood panel	@$75	$75
3	3x	sky alert bells	@$20	$60
4				
5		Service & tune-up		$250
6				
7				
8				
9				
10				
11				
12		Total		$485

RECEIVED BY:

KEEP THIS SLIP FOR REFERENCE

TO: SANTA
FROM: MR. GRIMSBY, PORTAL ENGINEER
RE: SACK FATIGUE

MEMO

My attention has been drawn to the poor condition of the outer fabric of the sack on this run. Its inner layer is connected via a time—space portal, a wormhole to the Infinite Warehouse in the Santa Dimension, or you couldn't possibly carry the cargo of gifts to all the well-behaved children in the world. The wormhole is kept open by a powerful Wishful Thinking forcefield. While it is feared it will collapse if belief in you falls below a critical mass, a more pressing problem is Sack Fatigue. If the hemp tears, the forcefield will destabilize and the entire sleigh could be warped to another galaxy. Major repairs are crucial. Please authorize repair budget asap.

JANUARY 5

Weigh-in day. Woke up with a heavy feeling in the pit of my stomach, which got worse when Mamma C. introduced a hi-tech Weigh & Say scale, sent to me by an anonymous 'friend.' It announced my exact weight, down to the last ounce, with a distinct note of disdain. I explained that the donuts must have had too many sprinkles this year but Mamma C. was not impressed. She talked about body mass, pinched over an inch and tutted, went on about expanding waistlines and health implications for the older man. It seems I am an endomorph, which apparently spells all sorts of trouble. No two ways about it—it's time for the new Santa regime.

Endomorph, moi?

Get off CHUNKY!

Find out who sent the talking scales.

MAMMA C.'S PLAN

- Strict diet—try goji berries
- Yoga
- Review work/life balance —less sleightime, more playtime
- Meditation
- Visualization?

Check if health
insurance covers
endomorphs.

My new yoga threads

those domes must
be tricky to navigate

JANUARY 6

Got a postcard from Eastern Ops saying all had gone well with the delivery of gifts in Russia—felt like dipping into my chocolate stash to celebrate—couldn't find any. Seems the regime has kicked in. Mamma C. has decreed that January should be dedicated to a fitter, healthier Santa, looser in body and mind. Think she has been to the mobile library again.

JANUARY 7

Smoothies for breakfast and salad for lunch. Cookie cravings at an all-time high.

JANUARY 10

Yoga day. I don't think my body was made for this kind of exercise. Should endomorphs really stand on their head? It can't be safe.

JANUARY 15

Mastered the Sun Salutation sequence. But Downward Facing Dog pose is a real challenge. My beard keeps getting caught under my hands and is really painful.

JANUARY 20

Mamma C. pulled out all the stops and made me a new outfit for my yoga exercises. I love it!

JANUARY 26

Hey ho (ho ho), new week, fresh start; I've lost an inch or two off the middle but no actual weight loss. It must be all turning to muscle. Could goji berries and yoga be making a difference?

JANUARY 27

All-day Workshop workshop at the Lapland plant, convened by the Executive of the Amalgamated Little Helpers and Yuletide Craftsmen Union; it will be a great opportunity for some management/workforce crossover—and they do a great working lunch.

Workshop Workshop
January 27

1:00 pm Lunch
* foie gras de rouge gorge
* roast ox en croûte with potatoes dauphinoise and carrots Rudolph
* cheeseboard
* profiteroles, cheesecake, chocolate cream pie
* fruit, nuts, brandy

WORKSHOP WORKSHOP
JANUARY 27

8:00am Breakfast
8:30am Thinking Outside the Toybox—lecture
10:00am Refreshments
10:30am The wheels come off! Dealing with the unexpected—masterclass
11:00am Square peg in a round hole? 'Fitting in' exercises—group improvisation
12:00am The Tinsel Curtain: sinister threat or trading opportunity?

JANUARY 28

Get Simkins in Weights and Measures Compliance to
check those scales; how can a person put on ten pounds
in a day? I didn't even have the cheesecake. Must do
an extra hour on the treadmill before the weigh-in.

JANUARY 29

Had to take the sleigh back into maintenance;
accounts won't be pleased—still some issues with
the Santanav. The tech team recalibrated it and
installed a new Disambiguation Drive, to avoid
embarrassing glitches of the Paris Texas/Paris
France type—had to smooth a lot of feathers
over at Père Noël S.A. They still bring that one
up and it's been five years! For a small franchise,
they sure are touchy. Still, at least I'll be able
to take the old girl for a test run at the New
Mexico facility. It would be so much easier if R & D
would just get on with the cloaking device—then I could
take her up whenever I wanted without worrying about
being seen. I'm tired of having to book New Mexico and
pretend we're a UFO—as far as I'm concerned, we are
certainly identifiable, and
I resent being called an
object!

Howdy, Pard'ner!

Make a call to R & D.
 Look for other test
run options: Siberia,
Antarctica, Himalayas—
could pop in on Yeti?

JANUARY 30

7:30am Nutritionist; take samples.   CANCELLED.

JANUARY 31

Had the old anxiety dream about a toy—this time it was a talking hotdog—coming at us from out of nowhere, demand for it going stratospheric, the workshops unable to fulfil and failing to deliver. That's two months earlier than last year. Had to break into my secret chocolate coin stash—some get wedged in the sleigh and I can't exactly let them go to waste...

FEBRUARY 1

Not well. :-(

Eat me...

FEBRUARY 2

8:00pm Rudolph and I are attending the fundraiser dinner at the Society for Distressed Reindeers. I'm giving the keynote speech. Better double check in case there's anything in it that could cause upset; the Group for Ungulate Rights (GUR) is getting very litigious these days.

SDR
SOCIETY FOR DISTRESSED REINDEERS

SDR would like to invite you to our annual fundraising dinner

details overleaf

SPEECH NOTES

Dear friends... my honor and privilege..

- What we owe the reindeer nation...
- avoid mention of hoof splitting and late grain payments
- 'putting antlers together
- loyalty... hardwork... usual stuff...

FEBRUARY 3

I was complaining today about missing my old
assistant, good ol' Mrs. D., when Mamma C.
sat me down and said I needed a more
21st-century P.A. to handle the PR side.
Turns out she'd already hired someone and,
sure enough, today I met Byron Poindexter
from The Hallowe'en Group. He's pretty hot
stuff. Helmed the Vampiric Special Effects
Department for two years after getting an
M.B.A. from Harvard. He seems
to have hit the ground
skating and I couldn't find
anything on my desk this afternoon,
but hey. PS—Rudolph looked very
snazzy last night—his nose seemed
to just light up the room.

Nicholas F. Christmas,
PhD, M.B.A., Harvard
(in my dreams!)

FEBRUARY 5

Swatches for the new suit in!

Hmmm

Too folksy?

Loving the
stripes!

A bit shiny...

ugghh!

FEBRUARY 7

Poindexter is on fire—he's already bringing in some media consultants—Team Tannenbaum—to upgrade Santacorp and ensure a year-round media presence. Bit worried—he showed me their website and it's headed with 'All press is good press.'

TANNENBAUM
BRAND STRATEGISTS

TEAM

ALL PRESS IS GOOD PRESS

'See the wood for the trees'

FEBRUARY 8

Well, Team Tannenbaum is certainly full of ideas... or full of something. They think we need to keep a high media profile all year—not just in the run up to C-Day. The one with glasses said that we were losing a sizeable market share just relying on old habits and tradition. Market share of what? Mamma C. and Poindexter seemed impressed. The guy has 'calendarized' them, whatever that means, for breakfast meetings once a month. It better be a good breakfast.

TANNENBAUM TANGENT: Our first meeting with Santa, and we had to combat a very negative vibe; it was difficult to persuade him that 'not fixing it if it ain't broke' is not an option in the current hostile Gifts and Goodwill climate; he did not seem to realize the extent to which Easter Bunny Inc. had encroached on his patch. We now see that breakfast meetings were a tad naive... he seemed too distracted by the donuts.

FEBRUARY 9 MEETINGS

9:00am Accounts
10:00am Scheduling
11:00am Compliance
12:00am Working Lunch with Steering
Committee for the Implementation
of Information Cascade Directive
(Distribution and Fulfilment)

Ho, Ho, Hum..

FEBRUARY 10 *Will you look at this?* ↘

🌲 TEAM TANNENBAUM

We feel that Santa's 'sack' is a tired cliché and doesn't put across the hip new image that Santa needs if he is to retain his edge.

We have some exciting ideas on the table—including using all that exterior sack cloth for something useful, a logo at the very least—and request that we agenda them for our next meet. Think 'man bag!'

Hmmph!

FEBRUARY 11

250¼lbs! How did that happen?

6 cinnamon donuts = 1650 kcals. Who would have thought?

FEBRUARY 12

Why is it getting so hard to tell naughty from nice? IT have had to reboot the Naughty or Nice database—again. That's the fifth time since C-Day and already Buxton in Indexing is giving me grief. Wish we still used the card system—I swear the Tooth Fairy is trying to pull a fast one on us. I'll use the time to get back to some old-time toy designing.

A couple of mine from the archives!

TO S. CLAUS: As you know, the Tooth Fairy Surveillance Group was requisitioned last year to take control of bringing the admittedly antiquated Naughty or Nice (NoN) Database into the digital age. As you also know, we've had a few teething problems lately (ahem), to say the least. Can we discuss?

Yours faithfully,
A. Buxton, Head Indexer, Naughty Division

FEBRUARY 13

Time's slipping past and I'm just not keeping up. Mamma C.'s sore that I didn't get home till late: she's threatening me with a life coach if I don't learn to manage my time better. I know I'm neglecting the reindeer. Need to boost their energy levels.

SLEIGH **SLIM**
North Pole

Just a little reminder from your local branch. We haven't seen you for a while, and we worry. Our next meeting is February 15—hope you can make it.

Dorothy

FEBRUARY 14

I know, I know, this is Cupidity Inc.'s big payola day, and I shouldn't be tossing dimes into a rival's hat, but Mamma C. would have my head if I didn't do something. I've planned a surprise romantic dinner for two tonight, with the finest pink champagne, roses and candy—maybe even a sleigh ride for deux!

FC

MC

FEBRUARY 15   Sleigh Slim meeting 7:30pm

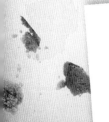

TANNENBAUM TANGENT: Cupidity Inc. is the perfect example of Santa 'missing a trick'. This niche subsidiary of rival conglomerate Metamarketing Ops would be perfect for a Santacorp take over, but try telling that to Mr. Wine and Dine...

FEBRUARY 16

Always feel braced after a Sleigh Slim meeting; should try to go more often. It's hot chocolate with skinny milk from now on and only one marshmallow in my treat allowance... and maybe some whipped cream.

SKINNY DELIGHT
1 cup hot water
2 tsps no-cal instant chocolike
½ cup whip skinny soya milk

FEBRUARY 18

Sticky meeting with IT and CEO of Tooth Fairy Surveillance Group (who knew she had a husband? She keeps that one under her bonnet). I zoned out a bit, and heard them discussing this crazy Self Assessment form. I've always relied on the kids to say if they've been good or bad, and some background checking with the parents when I feel they're not being straight with me (you gotta have a nose for this kind of thing; it's not for novices), but Poindexter thinks this is sloppy and there might be trouble with new Accountability and Fraud legislation. What on earth are 'self-certified behavioral tendencies.' Can't anyone just be naughty or nice anymore?

TANNENBAUM TANGENT

Go Poindexter! This form was to be completed online and submitted by October 31 at the latest, otherwise the applicant would be penalized by one gift for every week overdue.

Form NoN/1

YOUR REFERENCE:

OUR REFERENCE:

DATE:

PART ONE: Information About You

GENDER Boy/Girl

DATE OF BIRTH

AGE

STATUS

[ ] Only child
[ ] Eldest child
[ ] Youngest child
[ ] Middle child
[ ] Orphan
[ ] Stepchild
[ ] Adopted

If adopted, please indicate
whether adopter is a celebrity

How many parents do you
have on site?

[ ] 1
[ ] 2
[ ] more than 2

How many parents do you
have offsite?

[ ] 1
[ ] 2

PART TWO: Your Goodness Factor
Have you been consistently good
since December 26 in the last
Christmas year?
If so, please indicate how good
by checking one (1) box

[ ] Quite good
[ ] Satisfactorily good

[ ] Good
[ ] Extra good
[ ] Supernaturally good

Have you been bad?

Have you been consistently bad
since December 26 in the last
Christmas year?

If so, please indicate how bad by
checking one (1) box

[ ] Not very bad
[ ] Quite bad
[ ] Bad
[ ] Really Bad
[ ] Bad to the bone

REFERENCES
Please insert the names and
contact details of two witnesses
(not your parents) who can
corroborate your claims

Witness 1

Witness 2

Please indicate that to the best of
your knowledge the information
on this form is correct by typing
your NoN code in the box 1225.

The beard in all its glory...

Chris
Wayne
Gwen
Diane
Lisa
Mike
Gavin
Bren
Sam
Jenny
Tom Baker
Yasmin Ma

FEBRUARY 21

Am I the only one here who thinks Poindexter's naughty/nice form sucks? After demolishing a six pack of chocolate peanut butter cups, I came up with a genius plan to stall him—make him set up a focus group to test consumer reaction before going ahead with it. I can beat him at his own game after all!

FEBRUARY 23

Went down to see the reindeer and reconnect a bit. Something's bothering Rudolph—his nose was damp and more of an orange color. He said it was a cold.

FEBRUARY 25

Beard Day. Today was the day it all came off. Down to the wood. The bi-annual harvest. I do it to promote a full bushy model for C-Day. Know it makes the hair grow back stronger, but, like always, I miss the old ZZ Top look. The barber had a good haul this year—two dollars, six quarters, that decoration we couldn't find when we took the Christmas tree down, and half an Oreo. Emergency beard extensions are on standby for any unscheduled early appearances.

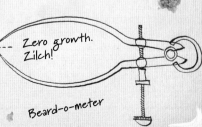

Zero growth. Zilch!

Beard-o-meter

FEBRUARY 26

I hate the first week of regrowth. Itchy! Mamma C. suggested I use some of the products from the 'Spruce-up Santa' kit sent over by the Tannenbaums this morning, but I refused. Lots of bottles in a smart leather bag with my initials on don't fool me. What's 'antioxidant cleanser', anyway? Sounds more like something for the sleigh. Auto bronze gel for men? They CANNOT be serious.

Who needs bronzer?

TANNENBAUM TANGENT: Of course we were serious! Santa at that point had a serious image problem. As anyone who's anyone knows, the only way to keep on top is to keep moving, and that means keeping on top of your image. Santa needed a makeover, and it was our subtle way of telling him that. Of course, he was still in denial...

FEBRUARY 28

Poindexter told me the Tannenbaums want to schedule all meetings for 11:00am from now on. I mean, really. I was just getting to enjoy power breakfasts, and now they are seriously eating into my brunch time. Those women really do take the biscuit.

FEBRUARY 29

~~Clans Sleigh Slim meeting~~ TOO BAD...

Meeting cancelled due to slight fire damage to the hall.
The previous meeting is Arsonists Anonymous, so go figure.
Still wasn't off the hook though—Mamma C. sprung a
weigh-in on those wretched talking scales. Surprise,
surprise! It told me, in the happiest voice I've heard
yet from them, that I had lost
a pound! Mamma C. said—rather
meanly I thought—that my beard
may account for a large part of it...

Beard clippings

MARCH 1

11:00am Tannenbaum meeting

♠ TEAM TANNENBAUM

AGENDA

11:00am Review need for focus group for Naughty
or Nice (NoN) Self Assessment PR, strategy,
challenges and rewards.

12:45pm Synergy with Cupidity Inc.: a match made
in heaven?

AFFIRMATION 2:
Don't lose your
head when all around
are changing theirs.

MARCH 2

Mamma C. away all week in Greenland. Woo hoo!
Time to crack open the cookie stash... She's off
to some crazy spa the Tannenbaums recommended.
Apparently it does the best mud packs on the
planet... but more importantly, it's Santa Time!

MARCH 3

I know she left me notes, but I don't know how to work
the microwave. Might pop round to Mrs. D.'s for supper
now. I've managed to completely demolish almost all my
cookie stashes. Must
do refills tomorrow.

Dearest S.

Off to Greenland now! Can't wait to
do the ice baths and hot stones the
Tannenbaums were going on about.
Be sure to eat your five portions of
vegetables a day—I've prepared all
the meals in advance for you—they're
labeled in the fridge, by day and with
instructions on how to cook them in the
microwave. REMEMBER TO TAKE THE
PLASTIC WRAP OFF THE DINNERS after
taking them out of the microwave.

Please don't forget to go to your Sleigh Slim
meeting on March 6—I've told Dorothy to
expect you.

I'll phone to let you know what time
I arrive back at the airport.

XXX

MARCH 4

Couldn't get
microwave to work.
Asked Rudolph to
help, but his hooves
couldn't handle the
push-button controls
and he scratched
the door big time.
Getting Production
to make another—
hope they manage
it in time.

Greenland
the coolest place on earth

MARCH 5

Called the Elf Line and
one of the technicians
came round and showed
me how to use the
microwave. What is it
with the transparent
stuff that Mamma C.
puts on top of her dishes?
Too chewy for my liking

Vegetable portions x 5
= positive result.

MARCH 6

~~2:00pm - Sleigh Slim meeting~~

Felt sick. Too ill for Sleigh Slim

MARCH 8

Mamma C. back tomorrow. Serious panic here at Yule Lodge. The vacuum cleaner wouldn't suck up all the crumbs and the den carpet was covered in pizza stains. Told Poindexter to get round here fast. Within an hour, he had a steam cleaner here—talk about a close call! I also made him take away some of the meals left in the freezer by Mamma C... I have so much to catch up on this week, and I can sense some disquiet among the reindeer. I think Dancer might be depressed now, too. I need Mamma C.'s calming influence. But maybe not first thing tomorrow.

Itching like crazy!

13mm

Beard-o-meter update

MARCH 9

Mamma C. got back early this morning. She looked radiant. Briefly. And then it was a bad day all round. She was not impressed by my attempts at stain or weight removal, and found half a cookie under a couch cushion. Agreed to go to the next Sleigh Slim meeting, no matter what.

Mamma C. brought this back-bit too Zen for me →

Greenland Spas

Discover a cool, brand new you

SLEIGH SLIM
North Pole

March 11

Dear Santa
We missed you at the meeting last week. We trust you managed to feed yourself in your wife's absence.

Dorothy

MARCH 12

Weigh-in by Mamma C. on talking scales. Have put all the weight back on. Slight beard regrowth but nothing to speak of. Deep in the doghouse. When quizzed by Mamma C. about what I had eaten while she was away, I said that last week seemed a bit of a blur, which wasn't wholly untrue. I said that Mrs. D. made me some great salads... I was pretty sure there was salad on the table. I wasn't going to mention the delicious spaghetti and meatballs. But then she phoned Mrs. D. and didn't speak to me for the rest of the day.

Arrf!

MARCH 15

Doi-ng!

Spent the evening with Dancer trying to cheer him up. Rudolph joined us and we reminisced. I had forgotten how we clipped Big Ben that time. I'm sure that one of the sleigh bells is still lodged on the top of the tower—I can hear it jingle when I whizz past each year. I felt much better after spending time with the boys and even Rudolph seemed more himself. Had an early night. Cookie count = zero. That's teamwork for you.

MARCH 16

The minute I woke up I could feel in my bones that this was going to be a difficult week. Poindexter rang to report that belief in me is at an all time low this decade. He is going to call the Tooth Fairy and ask for advice. We need to nip this in the bud or we will have serious trouble with the sleigh this year. No belief = no sleigh juice. Mamma C. says we should call the Tannenbaums straight away, but I want to think this through first. Poindexter said he has dealt with exactly the same problem at the Hallowe'en Group. Said within a month, he'd boosted witch belief by 220%. I am going to sleep on it. Let's see how the cookies crumble in the morning.

TANNENBAUM TANGENT: This incident revealed just how much we could help Santa with his global image and marked a real breakthrough in what had been a rather tricky relationship so far. PR and ID are what we do. And nobody does it better. Slamdunk. Go, Team T.

MARCH 17

Didn't sleep a wink and couldn't think of a rescue plan.
I was fretting so much Mamma C. made me put a call
in to the Tannenbaums at 7:00am—the one with the
glasses sounded practically asleep, but they insisted they
were already at their desks. They suggested a 'Belief'
Conference in the Great Hall, attended by international
franchise delegates, with video coverage for those unable
to attend. I guess all the usuals will show up for a free meal:
Tooth Fairy, Easter Bunny, Père Noël and Sinterklaas never
refuse a networking opp. Maybe even Frosty? Or how about
ol' Yeti—he just doesn't seem to get out enough. Mamma C.
is already trying to figure out where everyone will stay.
I wonder if the Tooth Fairy needs a special pillow?

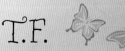

Dear Santa,

If you are reading this,
then you know that we
both exist. Looking
forward to seeing you
at the seminar. It should
be awesome.

T.F.

I eat, therefore
I am.

← Is this for real? It's
bad enough when
we have to invite
her to dinner.

GLOBAL UNDERCOVER RESEARCH TOUR

Mission statement: to research without
respite, investigate with rigor, and
report back in detail.

March 21 - London
March 22 - New York
March 23 - LA
March 24 - Sydney
March 25 - HK
March 26 - Bombay

Poindexter

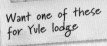

Want one of these
for Yule lodge

This is the life!

Near miss...

MARCH 19

Was hoofing it all week. Poindexter's brainwave paid off. He fixed up an action-packed multi-city tour of toy factories. I went disguised so I could check out how things are done elsewhere and pick up some useful tips on design, production, and efficiency. He pencilled me in for all sorts of meetings but I decided to see a few sights at a more leisurely pace. I took some extraordinary photos. I like this undercover stuff and the reindeer loved the trip. Dancer was on a high and Rudolph couldn't stop saying, 'Wow, did you see that?' Writing up a report for Santacorp—maybe I'll use invisible ink.

Night shots are getting better

Wonder if they can fly?

This spy stuff is a cinch. Might contact CIA to see if I can help them out.

Great detail on that bridge

MARCH 21

Mamma C. says that I am
a workaholic. She wants
to spend more quality time
with me and says I need
to learn to delegate more.
If I don't talk to Poindexter,
then she will. Maybe I
could delegate my exercise
program to him.

THINGS TO DELEGATE

- muffin sourcing
- yoga
- all Tannenbaum meetings

MARCH 22

Woke up to find Poindexter having a power breakfast with
Mamma C. Saw crumbs on his chin before he quickly wiped
them off—I'm sure they were those blueberry muffins
Mamma C. said had been eaten... He's already arranged
the focus groups for the Naughty or Nice forms and is
working in tandem with the
Tannenbaums on the Belief
conference. He's typed up,
edited, and distributed my
Secret Research report
and arranged a sleigh-
racing day for the
reindeer to keep them
cheerful. How does the
guy do it? His probationary
period is up soon. Will have
to think about whether
to give him a permanent
contract. I'll draw up a
list of strengths and
weaknesses.

Poindexter's good and
bad points
GOOD
- enthusiastic
- on time
- Mamma C. likes him
- organizational skills
- works long hours
BAD
- all of the above...

MARCH 24

I was reading the North Pole News while eating Mamma
C.'s organic porridge with no-fat milk when I spotted a
special offer for a week in Vegas in June, all inclusive. Rang
the number and got the last room at a reduced rate for
using my own transportation. June can't come soon enough!
Mamma C. and I can't wait for some downtime. I was so
excited I rushed to my room to try on my poolside outfit.
Mamma C. thought it would be fun to take a sneaky photo
of me and pin it to the
refrigerator as an
incentive to stick with
Sleigh Slim. She has a
point. Must go to the
meeting this week.
Or else just stay out
of the hotel pool.

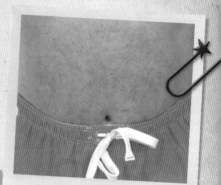

Time for Sleigh Slim

MARCH 25

11:00am Sleigh race

Fantastic day out. Dancer—for once—won all the prizes.
Rudolph's nose seriously out of joint. Teasing him about his
shiny nose only made it worse.

MARCH 26

Almost April already! Just thinking about
the workload sluicing down the chimney
towards us makes my bells jingle. Mamma
C. thinks I need a couple of sessions
with Guru O'Shaunessy, to calm down.
Dug out the mantra he gave me last
year; it's meant to soothe the 'pre-toy
nerves,' but I think my pitch is off-key.

Om

MARCH 28

11:00am Brainstorming with Team Tannenbaum

Shame we don't do the breakfast thing anymore. Hard to
distract yourself with nothing but branch water and a
kumquat. Apparently the donut budget's been axed. TT
(Team Tannenbaum!) say they have identified untapped
revenue potential; the deer and sleigh are idle for 364
days a year; the sleigh just depreciates and the deer eat
more than their own body weight in hay every two days.
According to them, it's a money pit. And of course we
have a global database, when it works. They suggest we
set up a bespoke courier gift service called SledEx. Must
say, they do work hard—they dimmed the lights, had
PowerPoint slides, music and everything (except popcorn).

I don't know. Seems to me that the deer do enough work in one night to deserve the rest of the year off, if the state of their hoofs after C-Day is anything to go by. And what would I tell the Tooth Fairy now? She's been wanting me to lease her the sleigh for ages.

SledEx

WE KNOW WHERE YOU LIVE

Tel: (00) 2512 1234
E mail: deliverance@sledex.np
www.sledex.np

SledEx is a wholly owned subsidiary of Santacorp North Pole.

WE KNOW WHERE YOU LIVE

Don't think Rudolph will go for this...

MARCH 30

11:00am Forward planning meeting this year's Stuffed Animal Distribution Strategy. Yum, they always have strudel.

MARCH 31
Dentist 4:30pm

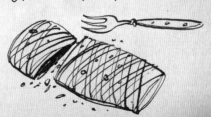

APRIL 1

April Fool's Day! Hid Poindexter's
paperclips and put sugar in his skinny
soya decaff latte. Ho Ho Ho!

APRIL 2

IT on the phone again. Another virus has got into the NoN
database! All the Charlies have been changed to 'nice'...
suspicious. Even if they clean it up, we may have lost data,
which means outsourcing it all to be ready for the October
deadline. Yawn. I haven't told them Mrs. D. is
secretly keeping the old card system up to
date for me. I'm paying her myself so it
doesn't show up on the books. Bottom
line: can't disappoint the kids.

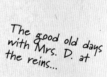

The good old days
with Mrs. D. at
the reins...

APRIL 5

2:00pm AGM Worshipful Guild of Gnomes
and Non-Elvish Operatives.
Hall of the Mountain King.

It's that time again. These meetings always make me
nervous, and I hate having to wear the full Red Suit
outside C-Day. The Guild drives a hard bargain—the
bosses know they have us over a barrel, but I like to
think that they would rather stay with Santacorp where
they can enjoy job security and work indoors than take
their chances out there in the harsh world of garden

ornamentation. We renegotiated the deal to a flat fee for this year, payable in three contractual tranches and a guarantee of a 1.5 percent increase in productivity.

The Gnomes' Guild Hall— impressive, don't you think? →

✴✳✝✶✳≢✝✝TTT

Worshipful Guild of Gnomes and Non-Elvish Operatives

BY MY HAND, THE FIFTH DAY OF APRIL

Let these runes be witness that The Worshipful Guild, who are bound by no contracts but those made by themselves or their descendents to the fifth generation, once more agree to renew their age-long fellowship with the High King of Santacorp and his house-earls. We swear by the Red Beard of Snorri, son of Sleipi, to come to the aid of Santacorp in their hour of need and battle with them side by side until all the toys are laid in their boxes. Only then shall our hammers rest.

♉

Lord Grumpi Grumpisson

APRIL 6

It's Grotto Design Submission Day. I used to enjoy this—we used to get some very high-class creations in, especially from Bloomies. Scale models, artist's impressions of the scene with actual people in it. Now it's all square lines and digital photographs; and don't get me started on the minimalist ones. Stainless steel Christmas trees? A single black ornament? Barb wire garlands? Christmas is about red and green and silver and gold and white. Does nobody read a brief anymore? (Note to self, stop getting grumpy; it only brings on the acid reflux.)

Mi grotto es su grotto!

SUGAR FREE

CHEWING GUM

All the chew, none
of the cookie coma

APRIL 8

Finally got to the bottom of the grotto pile, and narrowed
it down to ten official Santa-endorsed designs. Poindexter
wanted to make the selection using an algorithm he came
up with at Hallowe'en Group, but it was for the scariest
Haunted House design and I just don't think that's compatible.
Besides, I prefer to look through each one; finished a
family pack of double choc chip cookies (Poindexter had
three!) before moving on to the sugarfree Santa Gum
Mamma C. had the Candycane Workshop make up for me.
She's right; maybe I don't need the cookies—maybe I just
like to chew while I think.

APRIL 10

Went down to see the deer. They
always get frisky about now so I take
the soccer ball with me for a kick
around. Must admit an ulterior motive—
thought maybe I could run a few pounds
off; I had a few more choc chips than just the one pack,
and the Santacorp Tennis Tournament's coming up. Rudolph
seemed deflated again, but Blitzen looked like he was
having the time of his life.

APRIL 12

2:30pm Board Meeting

Bet Genghis Khan didn't have board meetings (more like bored meeting).

APRIL 13

Another anxiety dream, this time during my 1:00pm power nap on the office couch. I dreamt that I was trying to drive the sleigh through marshmallows and all the gifts were still on it and there was a big melting chocolate clock saying December 26, and my suit was getting tighter and tighter and I couldn't breathe, and we plunged over a ravine and into a freezing lake... woke up to find Poindexter spritzing me with Evian! He said I was yelling out 'Tally-ho-ho-ho!' and thrashing my arms around.

APRIL 14

We file with the IRS on April 15, so getting all sorts of grief from the accounts department; can I help it if the receipts get blown away? We do go at warp factor 25—what do they expect?
And they've rejected all my invoices for suit cleaning and repair. Apparently my mending bill is astronomical, and I am supposed to be more careful in the workplace. Like they could slide down so many chimneys and jackknife round those neo-Victorian angles and come out immaculate. Maybe I'll organize some kind of work experience for the bean counters, show them what it's like out there on the rooftops.

APRIL 15

7:30pm Sleigh Slim
Lost Olbs. Gained Olbs.
Could have been worse.

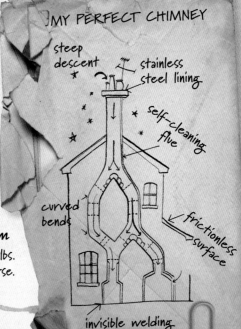

Snowhite ❄
LAUNDRY AND DRYCLEAN COMPANY

367973

$500 SANTA'S SUIT
REJECTED RECEIPT

MY PERFECT CHIMNEY

steep descent

stainless steel lining

self-cleaning flue

curved bends

frictionless surface

invisible welding
stainless steel lining

What a bunch
of vultures

APRIL 17

Thank goodness, accounts finally off my back. They've filed. You would think that Santacorp would get a blanket exemption, but you know what the IRS is like; they always want to know whether we are, strictly speaking, exporting, or just selling—it's just not that simple! And boy do they get snippy when I say that the goods are given away free and there is no delivery charge. And of course I don't have a salary! They audited us a couple of decades or so ago and found nothing; ours is just not a business model they understand. The North Pole Office is, of course, a tax-free zone, but that just means they watch it like hawks.

NOTE TO SELF: One day when I have time, I'll go through the NoN archives to see if I can find any IRS employee names. Bet they all signed up as nice children; bet they all sold their presents as soon as they got them and put the cash in an offshore tax-free fund. Should try and nip this kind of thing in the bud. We'll see who has the last ho-ho-ho.

Call Père Noël to see if he gets any better tax breaks than us.

APRIL 18

Must start to think more positively. Om-bauble-bauble-
bauble-ho-ho-ho and all that. I will look forward to our
holiday in Vegas! Sun, heat, free food! What's not to
like? Wonder if Rudolph would enjoy the slots?

Vegas here we come!

APRIL 19

Poindexter off on a training day. 'Advanced
Synergy Skills.' Practiced my golf putting
skills in the office with the new tea
boy (he's just an intern, hoping to get
into Tinsel Technology). He knocked
over Poindexter's bonsai plant—now it looks
like a Charlie Brown Christmas tree.

APRIL 21

Poindexter's back, more shiny and gung-ho than usual. Had to come on heavy to stop him organizing a think tank on our signature slogan, 'Ho ho ho.' He says we should think outside the gift wrapping, maybe add a 'Hee hee hee.' I told him it would be over Rudolph's dead body. He looked so disappointed that I asked him to explore maximizing the brand in non-traditional markets. I don't know what that means, but it should keep him off my back for a bit.

APRIL 22

The bonsai plant died—Poindexter looked like he'd lost his best friend. I brought him a replacement Blue Fir sapling but he didn't look impressed.

Looked at the catalogs for next year's electronic toys. Very depressing. I mean they just look like dull office stuff. I am pretty sure kids would like something with a bit more charm. I could design something better than these interminable black boxes. After all, I did my apprenticeship in the Finishing, Glazing and Varnishing Shop, and I'm pretty handy with a spoon chisel.

APRIL 24

Well, it took nearly all day, and I nearly lost a thumb, but I've made a prototype of what I've decided to call an S-box —I think it looks pretty good. Wonder

Haven't lost my touch with the old carpentry!

what it does? I'll send it down to R & D and
see what they can do with it. Hopes aren't
high though—still stinging from last year's
molten lava lamp rejection memo...

TO: S. CLAUS
FROM: MARTHA BEENGOOD, TOY IDEA
SUPERVISOR, ELECTRONICS DIVISION
RE: MOLTEN LAVA LAMP

MEMO

While this is a very good idea on paper, and
we appreciated your attempt to mold one out of
papier mâché, the implications of providing a
young child with a lamp that spewed molten lava
proved a step too far for our health and safety
department. We also had some burn issues with
the elves in the prototype room. The following
concerns also came up, which simply made this
product unsaleable—and downright dangerous...

- wouldn't switch on
- once on, wouldn't switch off
- shattered on impact

We tried our best to make these amenable to
toy worthiness, but I'm afraid this is another
one we will have to put in the rejected pile.

APRIL 25

The beard's past the itchy stage,
but now Mamma C. says I look like a
hobo, which she doesn't feel is a good
look for someone in my line of work.
Too bad, I thought I'd got quite a mean-
dude-Billy-Bob thing going on there.

28mm:
the hobo look

Beard-o-meter update

APRIL 26

Chased R & D about the S-Box thing I designed. I think it could fly off the shelves and could make Santacorp a fortune. It's gone to the Patents Office apparently. Must be good if they are thinking of trademarking it. Hmm... maybe they're starting to take my designs seriously. Poindexter was telling me about this great new product—clocks made of fruit. If they can do a clock, why not a phone? Will get onto it.

An apple a day, make your phone pay

MAY 1

May Day. Everyone was delighted with our new holiday. It was Père Noël's idea—his elves and helpers celebrate Labor Day on May 1 and the extra day of leisure has gone down very well here at the North Pole. I tried to call him to say how much I appreciated his neat idea but got his answering machine—he and Mère Noël are enjoying a boat trip down the River Seine in Paris today, complete with five-course lunch and Champagne tasting, or so I gather from Poindexter, who translated the message. That guy knows so many languages, even Romanian (he used to spend his summers in the Transylvanian countryside). Anyway, Mamma C. suggested a picnic à deux at Hot Springs Lake (I am picking bits up from Poindexter). She did the food—just mixed salad and lo-cal ginger beer and I did the rowing. We lost the oars a couple of times, but the water was toasty warm.

Check out
total immersion
French courses.

Tummy tightener
cream?

Wine tasting
seminar.

Ho-ho lâ lâ !

MAY 2

The factory was buzzing. It's amazing wha___ ___y off can
do. Smiley faces all round as I walked in. On___ ___weeks
to go before C-Day. Felt a panic attack comin___ ___nd
grabbed the nearest
snack—ten minutes later
I'd eaten a bag of cookies.
I think I'm orally fixated.
Wandered into the Chillout
Zone and found some elves
enjoying a real belly laugh.
My rowing muscles hurt
too much to join in so I
just laid down on the sofa
and caught a few
lunchtime zees. Found
this photo of Mamma C.
and me on my desk
this morning—weird.
Who took it?

MAY 3

Seeing those elves yesterday gave
me a great idea. I could set up a
laughter workshop at the factory
like the one Mamma C. enjoyed so
much at the spa. Apparently it's like
jogging for your insides, which sounds like my kind of
exercise! I am a natural—what's the word—'laughologist,'
so why not? Nobody can ho-ho-ho quite like me. I must
find that wonderful old Reverend Clement Moore poem.
He was a true friend.

A Visit from St. Nicholas
by Rev. Clement Moore in 1823

He had a broad face, and a round little belly
That shook, when he laughed, like a bowl full of jelly
He was chubby and plump, a right jolly old elf,
And I laughed when I saw him, in spite of myself...

MAY 7

Meetings, memos, decisions, dilemmas, figures and
forecasts, stats and spats... what a day! Poindexter and I
worked on my Retired Reindeer Foundation speech that is
coming up. Rudolph is to be a VIP guest and Poindexter has
arranged a PowerPoint presentation on fitness and hobbies
for the third age, antler care and reconstruction for the
elderly, and a cost-benefit analysis on private taxi work

for supplemental income. It got me thinking about my own future. What will I do all day once I retire? How will I stop myself from eating all the time? Will Mamma C. be able to cope with me 24/7? I know it's some way off but I feel I should work out some kind of retirement plan, maybe take up another hobby. My photography is getting better and better. I obviously have a talent for observation and perspective. I am thinking of arranging an exhibition of my best pictures in the North Pole Gallery, maybe even do some magazine photo-shoots?

Fabulous composition, tho' I say it myself

Great speed shot

MAY 8

Left message on AL's voicemail. Have a great 'fly by night' shot I want her to see.

Put in a call to Annie Leibovitz for advice.

Donner coming in
for his close-up

MAY 9

AL must be on a shoot. Just think—I could do one of those
too. I quite fancy wildlife photography in Africa. I've thought
of so many more great shots closer to home—reindeers at
play, reindeer food troughs, tracking wild reindeer, the
list goes on. I can see a whole new career for myself.

MAY 10

A bit disappointed today. No call from AL and Mamma C.
didn't think my photography plan was such a good idea.
She thinks I should focus more on my strengths. So now
I am thinking about writing a best-selling self-help book.
I have so much history and experience to share with
readers. Chimney logistics, present selection, reindeer
motivation... How to prioritize, delegate, keep calm under
pressure (I wouldn't mention the snacking). I could put
signed copies in people's stockings—let's see what TT
think of that for 'pumping myself up!' And then I could
branch out—I'm thinking coffee table books—'Christmas
Trees of the Rich and Famous.'

🌲 TEAM TANNENBAUM

9:00AM TANNENBAUMS' EXTRAORDINARY MEETING

'How to be Santastic'.
1. Power breakfast
2. Sleigh: pimp it up, green it up
3. Waist: size it up
4. Profile: pump it up

5. I ain't gonna give it up

MAY 11

This just arrived. Looks like tomorrow is going to be a BIG meeting. Ugghh.

POSSIBLE
BOOK TITLES:
* Christmas Trees of the Rich and Famous

* Chimneys A-Z
* How to Travel at the Speed of Light

* Creative Outdoor Photography
* Timeless Toys
* Beard-trimming

MAY 12

Team Tannenbaum arrived 30
minutes early. OMG. First they
made me eat maple syrup and
waffles and when my defences
were down thanks to the sugar
rush (now I know why Mamma C.

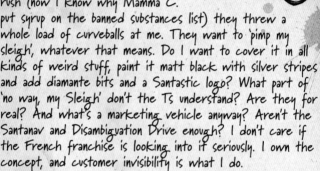

put syrup on the banned substances list) they threw a
whole load of curveballs at me. They want to 'pimp my
sleigh', whatever that means. Do I want to cover it in all
kinds of weird stuff, paint it matt black with silver stripes
and add diamante bits and a Santastic logo? What part of
'no way, my Sleigh' don't the Ts understand? Are they for
real? And what's a marketing vehicle anyway? Aren't the
Santanav and Disambiguation Drive enough? I don't care if
the French franchise is looking into it seriously. I own the
concept, and customer invisibility is what I do.

To keep them sweet I said I would look at greening up
our transport options. We discussed recycling reindeer
droppings—I had to keep reminding them they were called
fewmets. These aren't your average deer we're talking
about. We could even try and offload the excess, ahem,
output, and open up a new revenue stream. That's what
they do with guano, isn't
it? And we could add
solar panels to the
sleigh I suppose.
Think the Ts were
impressed by my 'green
sky' thinking

Fewmet fuel—get
Research team
to do a hands-on
harvest and
efficiency report.

And then they talked about my profile. I have to be bigger AND smaller at the same time, apparently. Bigger media presence, smaller Santa stomach. Maybe they've been talking to Mamma C.—that, or they've bugged the talking scales. I heard them mention the words I have been dreading for some time—personal trainer—but I tried to move the conversation along and told Poindexter to strike it from the minutes. I told the Ts about my bestseller ideas—they loved them and said they were going to suggest a book themselves (yeah, yeah)—a Santa memory book. I had to agree it was a neat idea. I'll do some research and come up with a few ideas. Feeling pretty nostalgic recently and it will be great to go through all the old photos in the attic.

Outcome = Income?

Find key to attic.

TANNENBAUM TANGENT: Okay, so this was a BIG agenda but if Santa was going to pack a punch out there we had to go in heavy. We had been treating him with kid gloves for just too long. Things were pretty chilly to start with but the waffles and maple syrup power breakfast went down well and by the end of the meeting, Santa was almost eating out of our hands. We had to give in on the sleigh-pimping—for the time being. Almost a home run. Victory for Team T.

MAY 14

Got a call from Rolf in Research. Turns out fewmet fuel is highly combustible. Feasibility vs. flammability study needs to be put in place or we could be in deep doo doo.

MAY 15

Winter few-ew-el

6:00pm Sleigh Slim meeting

Bad day. Put on 3lbs—how is that possible? Does each waffle weigh a pound? I think donuts must be much lighter. And I am bound to weigh more in the evenings.

← Beard's looking awesome here

MAY 16

Rummaged in the attic. Found some wonderful photos. I was pretty handsome as a young guy. Mamma C. was gorgeous, of course. And Rudoloph as a youngster. Move over, Bambi. He was soooo adorable.

Isn't he the cutest thing you ever saw?

Who's the Daddy?

Sponsorship—hmm let's investigate

MAY 19

Spent day in the attic again. Mamma C. unimpressed by the noise, mess, and general disturbance I was causing. Poindexter joined me and we sorted out quite a few administrative issues and factory problems up there while unpacking all the boxes of photographs and memorabilia. Thinking of putting a desk in here and making it my office. I'm used to dark spaces.

HEARTIEST

GREETINGS

Prancer or Prankster?

Those were the days

Buy desk for attic.

Buy bed for attic.

If you don't come out of the attic soon, you can move in there.

Your wife

MAY 20

Slept in the attic. Mamma C. definitely not happy with me. This memoir-writing business seems to be pretty tough on relationships, but all artists must make sacrifices.

MAY 23

Crisis at the factory. Poindexter said the computer had crashed, all the statistics had been lost and it looked like IT had forgotten to back the files up. Looks like Mrs. D. and her index cards are back in business! Mamma C. called it a reality check, as I emerged from the attic at last. She is probably right.

MAY 26

1902   1939   1951   1985   2002

Got in early (couldn't sleep, night sweats) and caught
Poindexter doing squat thrusts and lunges behind his water-
cooler. They were all a bit leaner and meaner over at
Hallowe'en Group and I suspect he's preparing to thrash
everyone at the Santacorp Tennis Tournament. It sure
would shock the elves out of their
complacency. Ten trophies in a row
doesn't mean you can rest on your
laurels. Note to self: have I got
time to shape up? Better make
today Last Danish Day.

Bye-bye Danish

MAY 27

4:30pm—acrimonious session with Warehousing. It was about
the Just-in-time system. The new divisions like it (it cuts
down on fire risk and theft), but the traditional workers
are antsy; they like to see a warehouse busting at the
seams in good time for C-Day; must say I agree with
them although I have to be impartial. It's like the secure
feeling you get when you open the fridge and it's full.
By jingle, I think I've just had an insight. Wonder what
Guru O'Shaunessy would think? Better schedule in a
session before my birthday.

MAY 29

Tried on my Vegas clothes. I think Mamma C.
might be right—a personal trainer would help
just to take a few inches off my waistband.
Will ask Poindexter if he can recommend anyone.

MAY 31

Needed to get out and breathe some polar night air, so
took the deer and sleigh out for a test run. Turned off
the Santanav and went by my whiskers like I used to in
the good old days. Looped the loop, went in to a half roll
with a twist, and came out with my hat still on! Yeeha!
Made me remember to ask Maintenance if we can get
the deer's hooves reinforced on the outside edge. Tried
out my new hoof oil recipe, but I think Prancer may have
had an adverse reaction. He spent most of the night
licking his feet.

HOOF OIL RECIPE

1 cup soya oil
1 oz crushed holly
leaves
1 tsp tincture of
mistletoe
1/2 tsp dried special
mushrooms
1 tsp ground cinnamon
3 drops Finnish vodka.

Oh boy! Found this in
the attic when I
was doing my memoirs.
It must be December
1893. What a night!

JUNE 1

Personal Trainer Session 7:30am

Mamma C. woke me up to make me
eat a banana half an hour before my PT
session. Must say I was not expecting a
lady. Felt a bit of a slob in the comfy
pants from No. 3 suit and that old T-shirt
from the 1985 'Just Say Ho' campaign. Holly
looked very slick in a dark green unitard. Said it's made
of something called spandex. I wonder if they do it in red?
Looks like it would be just the thing for chimney work.
Holly was great and soon had me zipping up and hollowing in
my abdominals, although I told her that I was strictly a
button and bulge kinda guy, which made her laugh.

Feel the burn!

JUNE 3

Still getting the night sweats. Only six months to go.
So much could go wrong. It's Poindexter's first year at
Santacorp. Om bauble
Mantra not really
working. Called Guru
O'S, who said I should
have a Focus Object.
I'm using one of the
snowglobes from last
year's surplus—it's got
a little me in it, and
I shake it then chant
while it settles. Cooled
down a bit. Took this
shot of my globe to
practice my close-ups.

I'm wasted

JUNE 5

Poindexter threw a hissy fit; apparently the sleigh was spotted by NASA. I was supposed to file the flight plans. Who knew? Mrs. D. always knew when I wanted to go airside without me having to say. Have promised I will let him know next time. Told him it wouldn't go on his record, and offered him a donut, but he just kept fiddling with his stress origami kit and staring into space. Luckily, just as I was about to give him the day off, TT called to scream at us about seminars and 'subliminal strategizing.' They were ecstatic. Whatever jingles your bell, I suppose. Poindexter was so relieved he immediately went off and co-ordinated the entire Santa Seminar Program three months early.

Santa spotted in June

Poindexter's origami tree

TANNENBAUM TANGENT: Santa seeing things through the TT lens at last! Just goes to show you got to have faith. We couldn't believe it when NASA called, and the National Enquirer ran the picture of the sleigh looping; needless to say, it's all over the web. You just can't buy this kind of media frenzy—and in June too, traditionally a dead time for the brand. Ring-a-ding!

JUNE 6

Spent whole day on celery diet. Blech!

Poindexter proudly holding his trophy aloft

Santacorp 'Mens' Singles Trophy

Ludo ergo Sum

JUNE 7

Poindexter and I thrashed the Tannenbaums at the Mixed Doubles! Must be getting fitter—I've never won anything before. Poindexter triumphed in the Mens' Singles. There was a bit of ill feeling as Leif Greenbaum, our Elf CEO of Safety and Security, usually wins. Some of the pixies lost money, but they got over it. Great day. Strawberries and cream and raspberry gingerale for refreshments, which means I had two fruits today without even trying.

SANTACORP TENNIS TOURNAMENT   Rules & Regulations **APPENDIX D**

BETS: rules state that only chocolate money is exchanged in any type of 'betting' transaction that might take place, due to lack of a gambling license.

MIXED DOUBLES: owing to the diverse nature of the Santacorp workforce, the term 'mixed doubles' is used to denote any mixture of players, male, female, elf, gnome, pixies, little helpers, anthropomorphic manifestations and, in some years, reindeer.

JUNE 8

Meeting with TT to debrief after the spy mission we had back in March. Wish I could leave it up to Poindexter, but I am afraid of what they will all decide without me. They brought ice cream out to the roof terrace. Thought I'd try to lighten the atmosphere, so wore a false beard and dark glasses and introduced myself: 'The name's Claush, Shanta Claush.' Did not get a laugh. Not even a titter. Those women can be so lemon-faced. Maybe I'll make it a condition of their contract that they come to my Laughology sessions.

Anyway, they have been analyzing the data we picked up on our espionage trip and are talking about output, prioritizing objectives, flexible supply line infrastructure, and aggressive discounting. Completely zoned out. My mantric snowglobe was in the other suit. Agggh! Woke up to find I'd inadvertently eaten Poindexter's ice cream as well as mine. Why can't we just carry on as normal? All the fun of the spying tour turned to dust; I'd never have gone if I thought we'd end up like this. I must put my boot down. I am not, repeat not, closing down the workshop and outsourcing everything. They want to turn it into a heritage experience, with all the best-looking elves dressed up in something they wore 200 years ago, messing around with toy hammers and stuff. Stiltskin and his crew have been running that workshop for years, and that is how it is going to stay.

TANNENBAUM TANGENT: Showing vulnerability at the tennis tournament was a bad idea! Santa insisted on keeping the traditional workshop as it is, even though our breakdown showed it could generate a healthier revenue by working as a heritage center and theme park, used on a year-round basis. He agreed we could continue to outsource TV and film tie-in merchandise, but would not move on anything else. We will regroup and restrategize.

JUNE 10

Personal Trainer 7:30am

All quiet on the TT front. I sure told them. Went down to see old Stiltskin, in case any rumors had reached the workshop; we played a few frames of pool and had a couple of root beers. Had a look at Prancer's hooves on the way back—seemed fine today; he may have a cinnamon-intolerance to the hoof oil? Try a spice-free batch.

JUNE 11

New fitness pants arrived. Bit tight.

JUNE 12

Got myself into the new pants but Holly did not show. Got a big shouty man instead, who says Holly had been relocated to deal with an outbreak of wrist strain in the Baby Toys section (it's all that tiny stitching). The new trainer says to call him 'Sarge.' He shouts at me so hard my beard blows sideways, and he's thrown away the vibroplate; says it isn't manly. No more laying down to mellow tunes; I had to run, jog, skip and then get down and give him twenty up and down things with my arms. He made me do star jumps for an hour and by the end of it I was as red as my new pants. He gave me a program to take home, but I couldn't see straight enough to read it. Barely made it to the canteen, and had the blow out breakfast, with double hash browns (begged them not to tell Mamma C.).

MODEL: Quickfit

COLOUR: BerryRed

SIZE: Santa 1

MATERIAL: Spangledex

FITNESS PROGRAM FOR N. Christmas

DAY 1:	Upper Body Workout
DAY 2:	Lower Body Workout
DAY 3:	Middle Body Workout
DAY 4:	Cardiovascular workout
DAY 5:	Core Stability
DAY 6:	Flexibility and Stamina
DAY 7:	Rest Day

In addition to Pre-warm up, Warm-up and Cool down exercises

JUNE 13

Woke up with a pain in my butt, in a muscle I didn't know existed. Could barely stand. Mamma C. massaged it with pine oil. She said it must be doing me some good if it hurts that bad. No pain, no gain, I suppose. Called up Sarge to find out what the muscle was.

Sore muscle = gluteus maximus. Like that helps.

JUNE 14

Sleigh Slim Meeting 6:00pm

Lost 4lbs! Result! Dorothy pointed out that I was still 2lbs heavier than this time last year, but I won't be down-hearted. Celebrated with a small helping of fries.

JUNE 16

It's my birthday next week. Aargh.

JUNE 17

TT called an extra meeting. Thought I might have put them off for a bit, but boy have those women got Bounceback.

JUNE 18

TT meeting 11:20am

TT say the figures from the sleigh ride incident were phenomenal; apparently I got a 1.4 billion hits. Is that good? So they want to do more of the same; we threw around some ideas—maybe a bootleg cell phone video from my b'day party (told them I wasn't having one). Sometimes I wonder if they have been at the hoof oil. They said that the biggest generator of viral flow on the web were kittens, and showed me a film of five little fluffballs in tiny Santa suits climbing stairs, balancing on christmas trees, falling out of chimneys, and kicking baubles around. They wanted to post it on YouTube tonight. It seems harmless, and Mamma C. loves kittens. I gave them the go-ahead.

aaaawww!

TANNENBAUM TANGENT: This was one of our best, if we do say so ourselves, and got 100% client endorsement. Kittens are a number-one hit on YouTube and MySpace and the strategy behind this fantastic idea was to flood the web with small felines in corporate ID; no need for a logo; it is a foolproof way to bring the brand to the forefront on a 24/365 basis—on a very low-fat marketing budget. Bonus time n'est-ce-pas?

JUNE 19

It's the Beautiful Reindeer Competition tomorrow—a morale booster for the deer and a fun teambuilding day for the workforce before we all get down to gearing up for C-Day. But Poindexter has been fielding complaints. Some of the team think it's demeaning, and others think it is speciesist. Poindexter put out a statement saying it was in compliance with new guidelines on positive discrimination, so we'll go ahead anyway. Trouble is, some of the deer think it's divisive—they always think Rudolph has an unfair advantage.

JUNE 20

The weather was fine. Otherwise, it was a disaster. We'd just got going on the Shiniest Hooves Category when the stage was invaded by protesters from SPORT (Stop Patronizing Our Reindeer Team) waving banners and shouting; one of them pinned a badge on me and it all got very heated. We had to cancel the Best Antlers in Show section,

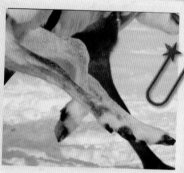

This is all we got from the professional photographer...

which upset poor Comet—he had a real chance of winning this year. The 100-Yard Sleighless Dash ended in a photo finish between Dasher and Dancer, who are no longer speaking. Poindexter had booked a professional photographer (I was too busy to do it myself), but all she managed was Vixen hoofing Cupid before the big stampede smashed her equipment. Will have a rethink for next year.

THIS DEMEANS DEER

JUNE 21

Three days to 5, 4, 3, 2, 1...
my birthday and
I am getting very nervous.
Happens every year, I hate it,
always want to just crawl in the
sack and get lost in another
dimension. But I am head of
Santacorp and it is a marker
for everyone else that we are
halfway through the year. Only
six months to C-Day! I wonder
what presents I will get.

JUNE 22

Pre-birthday session with Guru O' Shaunessy. He keeps
telling me to live in the now, but my core business is
anticipation, and some of it rubs off. He advised me to
up the number of mantras I did per day, and we did
some visualization work with the snow globe.

JUNE 24

Beard update: four
months now and
it's got past the
sticking out stage.
I am now into the
distinguished
master craftsman
phase and still don't have to plait it or
wear a snood when working machinery.
Gave it a bit of a trim—don't want a
bad beard day tomorrow.

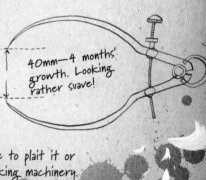

40mm—4 months'
growth. Looking
rather suave!

JUNE 25

HAPPY BIRTHDAY TO ME!

Woke up feeling gloomy. I know I am technically immortal, but suddenly feel a million years old. I can't help but start to wonder: what's the point? Sometimes I think that I wouldn't mind if everyone just stopped believing in me and I could get on with life as a private person. Tried to go to my Happy Place with the snow globe, but it was closed. Had a slice of strawberry cheesecake with my breakfast coffee (hey, it's my birthday) and felt a bit better. Then Mamma C. threw me a surprise party! Everyone came, even the Tannenbaums, but apparently Holly couldn't make it, since she's been seconded to the Hawaiian Office (didn't know we had one). Poindexter plays mean guitar (is there anything that guy can't do?) and we did a blistering session of 'Deck the Halls'...

WHAT I GOT FOR MY BIRTHDAY

* from Mamma C.— six more sessions with Sarge
* from Poindexter— The Rough Guide to Las Vegas
* from everyone— the workforce clubbed together and bought me something called a BlackBerry. Looks lovely. I'm sure Poindexter will explain it to me
* from the Tannenbaums—a Team Tannenbaum motivational desk calendar, with a positive thought bubble for every day

Rudolph admires the cake

Mamma C. gives the maracas a workout

GREAT CHIMNEY MOMENTS

Graceland, 1957. My first
visit to the King's new home

Dakota Building, NY, 1900. Will
you look at that brickwork?

View from the bottom of George
Lucas's chimney, 1977

The White House, 1993. Chelsea
left me a home-made cookie

Ohio, 2001. Wedged for 14 minutes. Christmas almost cancelled

Merry Pranksters at work in San Francisco, California, 1964

$$E=MC^2$$

Albert Einstein's chimney, 1905. In the presence of genius

First shot using a timer. Tricky ₃end in Tucson, Arizona, 1999

Mamma C. is organizing an exhibition of my work in the Little Arctic Salon so I've been looking through my chimney collection, digging out some of my favorites. She says it's better to have a few select works than a whole wall full of mediocrity. I've got some great ideas for the canapés at the private view.

JUNE 26 ⭐ -3!

DON'T FORGET
- beard trimmer
- sunblock for head
- cacti ID booklet
- best buffets in Vegas guide

VEGAS WARDROBE—
POOLSIDE & STRIPSIDE

SHORTS: Bermuda, red and white polka dot x 1

SHIRTS: Tee, red and white stripes x 1, Ho tee x 1, Long sleeved, red x 1

PANTS: red x 1, blue x 1

Dark sunglasses: x 3

Ho hat: x 1

DRESS SHOES: black x 1 pair

CLOGS: red x 1 pair suspenders

Crisis. Three sleeps till Vegas and excitement only just under control through a mix of 'om bauble' five times (omm...) and donuts twice (mmm...) to calm down—or was it the other way around? Poindexter called to say that they are still having trouble with the NoN database—now he's worried about unscrupulous pirate viral-marketeers and IT is still querying the back-up status and possibility of outsourcing. I didn't understand most of what he was saying —what would pirates want with the database? He looked dreadful so I put in a call to Mrs. D. to have the cards ready for my return from Vegas. I told Poindexter that I would sort it and he gave me one of his 'I don't remember seeing you at Harvard?' looks. He probably thought I had been sniffing hoof oil.

Lake Michigan, 1920

JUNE 27

 -2!

Rang Mrs. D. and had a lovely chat about retirement. Must say a little bit of me envied her but I would need more than book groups and bake-offs. She says she misses making me my marshmallow muffins with lo-cal sprinkles so I put in an order for post-Vegas. I am bound to lose weight on vacation. All that walking up and down the Strip will do me good and the sun is sure to sweat off a few cals. I can't wait to catch some serious rays.

Measure Rudolph's head.

I don't think so...

Had to call Mrs. D. back to ask her to get the cards out. Neither of us could remember the code for the foolproof safe I designed for them but it will come to me. My mind is too full of Vegas. Got a great present idea for Rudolph.

JUNE 28

Woke up with a start to the music from Presley's 'Viva las Vegas'—Poindexter must have fixed me a new ringtone for my cell. Mamma C. not impressed—by the theme tune or the time—6:30am. The Ts were on the line (hellooo, don't they know we are going on vacation tomorrow and need to stock up on zees? Even the Prez gets time off, doesn't he?). In my dreams, I was an industrial spy working out how an apple turns into a phone and a pea pod can play music. I was pretty close to working it out and then those women start shrieking at me. No wonder Leonardo da Vinci didn't invent the cell phone. Anyway they said they had a fantastic idea and needed to come round AS SOON AS POSSIBLE to tell me ALL ABOUT IT. Those women can really shout. Told them we are leaving tomorrow night and to come round later on.

Figure out how to put phone on mute.

TANNENBAUM TANGENT: It was just sooooo exciting. We were having a Pawpaw Pow-wow—our new concept for gray-cell red-eye thinking with power juice (we're going to try it on Santa after his vacation) and just had to call him. We had been watching a nature program on the park around Mount Rushmore the night before and it hit us both at the same time. Kapow! Let's put Santa's head on the Presidents' Memorial. You don't get much of a bigger profile than a 60-foot sculpture in South Dakota with a video link—not everybody needs face time. We couldn't wait to tell Santa. Okay, so it was a bit early but we needed to move fast. We didn't want Bigfoot's PR guys getting in first.

JUNE 29
9:00pm Departure for Vegas

V-Day!

All packed and ready to go. STV all solar-powered up
with new stealth facility charged—hope it works. The Ts
arrived and were both talking at once so it was hard to
work out what the BIG IDEA was. But when they told
me, I froze. By George! This was one crazy marketing
concept. They had even done a mock-up for us, with my
head in place. All too much to take in. Supersize Santa.
Rock on...I felt dizzy, like I suddenly had vertigo. Would
I have to pose? It could take months and we are coming
up to my busiest time. Do I really want to be that big?
Mamma C. said we would talk about it in Vegas but we
needed to get going. Promised the Ts we would keep
the cell phone on, but asked if they could avoid calling
before dawn broke next time. Set the Santanav to go
via South Dakota on the way home.

If the cap fits...

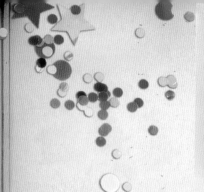

Move over Annie Leibovitz

JUNE 30

Landed safely on the Strip at 2:00am and were in our hotel room in what seemed like no time. A slightly bumpy ride to Vegas—the solar-powered engine failed a couple of times and we had to wing it over the desert—but it was incredibly beautiful by moonlight and I took some great shots. I feel confident we can sort the transport hiccups and Poindexter said there were no sightings on YouTube—don't know whether that's a good or bad thing anymore!

Apparently he'd been trying to reach me on that new Blueberry I got for my birthday—he'd left a message at the hotel when we got there. Said he keeps sending me e-mails, messages, and photos—I can't open any of them. I had only just got to grips with my cell phone, let alone this thing! He called me a luddite. I try to be patient with his campaign for '24/7/365 Santability'—his newly coined term—but I can't help thinking how much easier letters are. They are my kind of core communication tool. When Mamma C. said we just need some space I hope she meant between Poindexter and us, 'cos we have got a whole week of quality coupletime together.

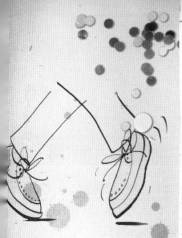

VEGAS TO-DO LIST!:

* Locate post office
* Buy blue suede shoes
* Research satellite office potential
* Try to crack the ~~blueberry~~ BlackBerry
* Buy show tickets—Elton?
* Call Mrs. D. with safe code
* Mt. Rushmore—thoughts?
* Keep and eye out for new toy ideas
* Ask TT about Vegas-style 'Welcome to the Fabulous North Pole' sign

The hotel room is great. There's an ice machine, a fully stocked tiny refrigerator and a trouser press. Two out of three ain't bad. I am going to like this place. Mamma C. insisted we go straight to bed but I couldn't sleep. I was buzzing. I felt really alive, like there was more oxygen pumping through my body than at home. Must be something to do with the latitude. My gray cells were working overtime. All kind of things kept hitting me, including the code to the safe—duh. And can you believe that the little fridge has a lock? Mamma C. must have hidden the key—in the end, I found an old cookie in my pajama pocket and did mmm..., omm... and some hmm... instead. Maybe I could set up a branch of Santa Inc. here—Poindexter could run it for a few months. I get the feeling he isn't the biggest fan of sunny climates though.

Safe—1225— of course!

JULY 1

First day of July. First real day in Vegas. First to get up. First in the pool. First at 'Betcha Can' breakfast and first-ever guest to eat four waffles in under three minutes. And I didn't feel sick afterwards. That was also a first. Mamma C. had a spot of sleigh-lag and didn't join me until after the pancake course, which was lucky on my part. Off to do a tour of Vegas!

JULY 2

Mamma C. snuck up behind me

By all accounts I passed out yesterday. We did a tour of Vegas after breakfast and I think I had a panic attack. It was all a bit too much like C-Day except in daylight. I started to worry that it was December already, that I had my timings wrong and was running way behind schedule. I may have also OD'd on maple syrup. I could see Paris, Monte Carlo, Egypt, and New York—all in daylight! It was like I was in a time warp. I asked Mamma C. to pinch me. And that's all I remember. Apparently I had to be carried back to my room by some friendly tourists, where I stayed for the rest of the day.

We took it easy after yesterday's little incident. Mamma C. said it was a combination of heat, maple syrup, excitement, insomnia, and stress. She gave me several of her looks. Persuaded her to join me on the Chocolottaslots I had found—three cookies in a row you could win a voucher for a two-foot wide chocolate cookie. It was fun but we lost every time, which made Mamma C. breathe a sigh of relief I think. Then had a gentle swim in the pool and caught a few rays. Felt so much better. Think I just needed to relax a bit. Mamma C. took a few photos for the scrapbook. The quality of light here must be quite different. You can see so much more detail in hers.

JULY 3

Felt hugely better today so we went for a gentle stroll at dusk after another relaxing day spent in the shade by the pool. Then we headed to the dancing show I had chosen from a brochure at reception. I wanted to surprise Mamma C... The music was fantastic, the showgirls amazing, the costumes something else. We were having a great time, holding hands, tapping our feet, and singing along and then the dancers decided to change costumes on stage. Maybe they don't have much room backstage? Mamma C. said we should leave immediately. I wanted to stay to hear some more show tunes but she wanted to get back to the hotel straight away. I managed to take a few photos of Vegas by night on the way home but Mamma C. seemed a bit flustered and in a rush. She was also very quiet—hope she isn't coming down with something.

Lights, camera, action. Maybe I could get into films...

Oh, what a night!

JULY 4

Independence Day and boy did Vegas celebrate—huge parades, fantastic fireworks, amazing light shows, incredible live music, delicious-looking hot dogs, and the biggest pancake I've ever ~~tasted~~ seen at breakfast. Mamma C. was watching me closely at breakfast this time—she says she is protecting me against excessive intake.

We were 'treating' ourselves (huh?) to a slice of watermelon by the pool when we were told there was an urgent call for us at reception. I thought it must be Poindexter with confirmation of tomorrow's arrangements but it was TT asking if we had decided about Mount Rushmore. Their timing is something else. I stalled them by saying Mamma C. and I had scheduled discussions for brand leverage after lunch (I am getting fluent in Tannentalk) but as I put the phone down, I knew the answer. They may want to pump up my profile but putting me alongside the presidents is just plain wrong. It would be like putting my head on the Statue of Liberty. They don't seem to understand boundaries. Must try to check out what the Ts were like as children. Will have a word with Mrs. D. and get her to look at the NoN cards. I think I know the answer already...

You call this a treat?

NO, NO, NO to Mt. Rushmore.

TT—naughty or nice?

Who's the King at photos now?!

JULY 8

Last day in Vegas but the BEST one ever. Mamma C. and I got hitched again—Elvis-style! We've been married forever and I thought we should celebrate so—where better than here? I have always been a huge fan of the King—he always left the best snacks by the fireplace—and thought it would be the perfect way to show Mamma C. how much I cared. I was even wearing my new blue suede shoes, which were a bit uncomfortable. My feet were obviously made for boots. I declined the wig and jumpsuit option and I couldn't do much about the beard but gave in on the sunglasses front for the actual event. Mamma C. looked beautiful and it was a fabulous ceremony. Elvis was amazing and offered us a ride back to the hotel in his pink Cadillac, with all three of us singing 'White Christmas'—I don't think he guessed who I was but some of the children we passed gave me quizzical looks like they knew. Poindexter and the team back home watched the ceremony via free Internet broadcast. Didn't tell the Ts about it—don't want them to be cruel about my blue suede shoes. Hope the ceremony doesn't make it onto YouTube.

JULY 9

HOLLYWOO

Back to North Pole
on overnight flight
with stealth facility for extra security, and
NOT via South Dakota. The STV was solar-powered up
to the max in Vegas and it was a smooth and romantic
ride. We sang Elvis songs all the way home and were
back in no time. Felt refreshed, rejuvenated, and ready
for the onslaught of the next few months. Vegas is a
natural battery charger. The warmth and the rays just
made my creative juices flow. How about 'what happens in
Vegas goes back to the North Pole.' Great slogan? Or
maybe 'I've got the Vegas Touch?' Eat your hearts out,
Tannenbaums. I can do my own PR.

JULY 10

Poindexter was there to greet us on our return along
with a mountain of memos, messages, meetings, developments,
disasters, and decisions. And a DVD of the ceremony—so
when do I get to watch that? He had feedback on things
that had gone well, things that hadn't, and lists for me
to do immediately, by lunchtime, by this evening, and even
while asleep. What is this guy on? Felt the Vegas touch
draining away...

Vegas or LA
next year?

Get Poindexter to
change ringtone to
'White Christmas.'

JULY 11

Snowed under. Overwhelmed. Exhausted. Want to go back to Vegas.

JULY 15

10:00am Sleigh Slim meeting

Minus 2lbs. Everyone was very impressed—and surprised I suspect. Even got a round of Santa applause. I told them I was very restrained after the first day's research into local dishes and that what goes on in Vegas comes off in Vegas.

JULY 18

11:00am Emergency Tannenbaum catch-up meeting

Refused to do meeting at 6:00am. Refused to do a U-turn on Mount Rushmore—what part of no don't they get? Wouldn't answer any questions about rumors of the Elvis wedding. Absolutely refused to consider releasing a DVD. It was a short meeting. Said I was too busy for lunch. They left looking a little shocked. Maybe I should just give them the sack—and I don't mean the one with the presents in it.

TANNENBAUM TANGENT: This was our worst meeting with Santa ever. He wouldn't budge on anything and even turned down lunch and pawpaw. Things were not looking good and we were worried Santa might end our relationship. We needed a new strategy. Nobody dumps TT.

HELP!

JULY 26

Poindexter at a 2-day Conference in Denver. My treat. Gives us both time to cool off after the Rushmore Debacle. Told him that TT are on notice, so I am not expecting anything loud from them right now. Had a nice quiet day looking at the Vegas snaps, but unfortunately slipped into a Mindless Eating trance, and before I knew it, got through three packets of Fig Newtons.™

JULY 28

Woke up to nature calling urgently. Fig Newton overload? Weird. Poindexter back. He was voted Man of the Conference and won the Laptop Challenge in the fastest time ever. What a coup—he never even got to the top three while he was with The Hallowe'en Group, and I've never seen him happier. Think he may have over-achievement issues.

To	b_poindexter@
Cc	
Subject	TWO DAY CONFERENCE , DENVER, COLORADO JULY 26-28. WHO MOVED MY STOLLEN?

Thank you for booking your reservation at the Cross Platform Strategies & Solutions for the Festive Sector event. We are pleased to confirm your place in the Downhill Laptop Challenge—Microtufts' most prestigious annual event. Please ensure that you read the rules of participation carefully, and bring this e-mail with you as proof of entry.

REMIT: Timed run on a 100-metre 45 degree dry slope.
EQUIPMENT: 1 personal organizer, 1 dry skinny latte, 1 x 15-inch laptop.
RULES: Participants must use laptop as transport down slope, latte in one hand, personal organizer in other. During run, one sip of latte must be taken, and one text message must be sent from personal organizer, composed of text pre-arranged by competition refs. Participants must be M.B.A.s.

JULY 30

Personal Trainer 7.30am

First of my birthday present sessions with Sarge. One down, five to go. He made me jog round the tennis court with him three times, then we did upper arm strength, to help me haul gifts up and down the chimney, apparently. Sweating at the end of the first half hour, so Sarge hosed me down. He invited me to one of his Iron Sarge weekends, complete with sweat lodge. Remember those from the shamans in Lapland when I was lad. Can't think of anything I'd like less, but smiled and nodded. Suspect he reports back to Mamma C. Wish Holly would come back.

JULY 31

I see Poindexter has scheduled in a meeting with TT for August 3. This had better be good.

AUGUST 1

Sint Nicolaes ('call me Sinterklaas') from the Dutch franchise dropped in after his annual cycling holiday in Norway. He needs to eat more—looks like a long streak of nothing under that robe. He has it so much easier. Arrives on November 15 after a short cruise from the Med; gets to ride a big white horse all round town, looking good for the ladies, then it's just a little light scattering of candies into clogs every night. He has his grunts doing all the Naughty/Nice paperwork, delivers a round of presents on December 5 and is back home in time for a leisurely run-up to Christmas Day. No wonder he looks so relaxed. But Mamma C. always enjoys his visits and he does bring cookies... he makes them himself, with special herbs. Haven't seen Mamma C. giggle like that for ages.

SPECULAASJES

1 1/2 cups flour
1 tsp baking powder
1 tsp nutmeg
1 tsp cloves
1 tsp mace
3 tsp cinnamon
3/4 cup brown sugar
1 stick butter
2 tbsp milk
a few drops vanilla extract

AUGUST 3

Meeting with TT 1:30pm

Very formal with proper coffee cups and all. They were very quiet, much quieter than usual, and even had quite a sensible idea. They want to set up a Trend Monitoring Unit; a 'dedicated task force to troll the net and surf the zeitgeist to find out what the Next Big Toy will be;'

if it works we could stock up in advance (goodbye just-in-time delivery!). Said I would think about it. Sucked back a strawberry milkshake when they'd gone, to calm the nerves. Ridiculous. I am Santa Claus! Tried some positive affirmations to the mirror—starting with: 'Who's comin' to town? That's right—Santa Claus'— but got too embarrassed.

AUGUST 4

4:00pm BlackBerry workshop with Poindexter to increase my 'Santability'. This is my 4th session, and I can already open e-mails—I still seem to send everything in uppercase though. Somehow lost the fur length-to-cuddliness ratio data from the Teddy Bear R & D Team but Poindexter has back up. This thing can even take photos. Tried it, but think I'll stick to the Polaroid for now.

My First BlackBerry Shot!

AUGUST 5

Postcard from the Noëls; they are spending all of August at their gîte in southern France. Mamma C. reminded me that we promised we would go. I just don't think we have the time. She got quite stern and said it would be a waste of our Vegas tans if we didn't go and we would come across as bad mannered. Then she got one of her headaches, so I went down to the stables and slept under the stars with Rudolph.

AUGUST 6

A quiet week—everyone's on vacation before we go for the big push. Only me and maintenance around. And the deer, of course. Always makes me anxious when I can't hear the sound of those little hammers going at it. Spent some time walking round the workshops, just getting a feel. Really must get going on the List. Which, of course, we will have to check twice. I've always written them out with Mrs. D. before— who knows how Poindexter will shape up. What if he buckles under pressure? Those skinny guys don't always know how to roll with the punches.

Me on my lonesome...

AUGUST 7

Held off the TT meeting. Played them at their own game and told them the focus group's results weren't quantified yet. They sent some delicious candies by courier. Absolutely must start on the List. Poindexter showed me how to make a spreadsheet that can interface with my BlackBerry. Very neat, but think I'll keep Mrs. D.'s old notebook system going, at least in private.

Sorry we missed you—
see you next week once
focus group has results.
TT

AUGUST 8

Mamma C.'s still got a headache, and my back is still sore from sleeping on hard ground. I had a look at the upcoming schedule; Poindexter's taking his power break at the end of the month, but I guess we can fit in a few days with the Noëls after all. Had Poindexter ask them if August 13–15 would suit. Can't find the mantric snowglobe.

AUGUST 9

Cleared my desk, unpacked crate of oat cookies (good for the brain) and sat down to generate the List. It will be a start, but must not expect too much of myself in August. Then remembered—Santa Soccer League starts next month and I haven't even organized the games. Got a good feeling about the Santacorp Sleighers this year; that player we poached from Easter Bunny Co. is dynamite. Reply in from the Noëls. Said they will be delighted to see us.

ARGGH!

SANTA SOCCER LEAGUE SCHEDULE:

GAME 1: Hallowe'en Group vs. Cupidity Inc.,
GAME 2: Easter Bunny Co vs. Tooth Fairy
GAME 3: Winner of Game 1 plays Santacorp?
Winner of Game 2 plays winner of Game 1
and Santacorp?

AUGUST 10

Mamma C. busy packing. She's doing the Sleigh Slim 3-Day Wonder Loss program, which seems to be mostly asparagus and boiled eggs without the mayo.

AUGUST 11

Elves back, and it's good to hear the whining of the
lathes again. Found Poindexter trying to reconfigure
workbenches down in the Educational Wooden Toys Shed.
Heard a distinct lack of happy whistling and got him out
just in time. Mentioned that the SSL games needed
arranging—that should keep him busy while I'm away.

AUGUST 12

Accounts Dept. Work Swap day

Took the beancounters on a Walk-in-My-Boots
experience at the Sleigh Testing Grounds. We
did take-offs and landings and controlled turning
circles. Then up to
Chimney Simulation Yard into
the full suits (in August, ho-ho
ho), down the chimney with a
full load, where they had to
sample simulated refreshment,
get out and get the sleigh
over to the next drop in the
standard time of 0.000013
seconds. Did my heart good
to see them sweating and
grimy, especially Persimmon
who's always querying the
cleaning bills.

Eat soot, beancounters!

AUGUST 13

Mamma C. repacked all her clothes again—I'm just taking my
Vegas gear. Poindexter calibrated the Santanav. Not looking
forward to seeing the Noëls—feel so large and sticky next
to them. I'll try to spend most of the time in the pool.

AUGUST 14

Arrived last night at the Noëls' residence—Notre Repos—
in time for dinner; must say they had put on a great spread.
Mamma C. hissed at me and whispered our secret word
when the cream gâteaux came round, but I pretended not
to hear. Père Noël was very charming and offered to
teach Mamma C. to speak French; and she is going
shopping for perfume with Madame Noël tomorrow.
Think I'm going to stick with the pool plan.

AUGUST 15

Pool plan failed, so it was shopping and sightseeing in
Cannes today. Lots of 'enfants' pointed and whispered, and
a couple asked for my autograph. Apparently there's a film
festival on here in May, and lots of Hollywood types have
yachts out here all summer;
they probably think I'm
some sort of movie star.
The Noëls have a yacht,
and we had lunch on it.
Boy, can they lunch. How
come he's so thin? I don't
see him attending any
Sleigh Slim meetings.

Le Floçon de Neige

Août 15

Déjeuner

Apéritif

Amuse-gueules

Fruits de Mer

La bourride avec sa rouille

Daube de Boeuf Provençale

Plat de Fromages

Tarte au Citron

Crème à la Coeur aux framboises

Le Café et petits fours

Digestif

AUGUST 16

Back from France. Birdstrike on the way back (came in too low over Greenland and forgot to recalibrate for extra weight) so sleigh back in the shop. The guano will wash off but I'm concerned about the beak damage; another worry I don't need. Mamma C. is staying on in France to polish her French, which gives me space to really focus and prioritize. Found my hammock right at the back of the closet (don't remember putting it there) and hung it by the stables. I find the rocking motion really helps to concentrate the mind.

AUGUST 17

The sleigh ran out of juice above the Indian Ocean and drifted down onto a desert island; when I came to, I was lying in a warm, swaying bed; a beautiful woman was stroking my beard... then I woke up and Rudolph was snorting into my face and licking my chin. Fell out of hammock. Looked up and saw Poindexter hovering impatiently with a ginko smoothie and his personal organizer, radiating zeal. He reminded me that I'd agreed to a breakfast meeting to confirm next week's handover protocol.

TO DO

* start recruitment drive for the Santa trainees
* are we self sufficient in wood, varnish, paint, non-toxic glue, kapok, fur fabric, plastic etc.?
* NoN database—speak to Mrs. D.
* test run the toy sorting machine
* roll out grotto program
* get the latest on conveyor belts—still sticking?
* novelty stocking fillers—ideas?

SLEIGH SLIM
North Pole

Sorry not to see you at the August meeting. Don't forget: September is a Self Renewal month when all th Sleigh Slimmers reaffirm their Slender Promise to themselves.

Dorothy

AUGUST 18

TT meeting 11:00am

Stayed austere. Fortunately, beard looking very authoritative right now.
We had black coffee and a citrus fruit medley, but then they brought out the big guns—raspberry cheesecakes, which I refused. According to their debrief, family values are returning with a focus on Amish style toys that look like Dad has spent months whittling them, there's a market spike in the niche irony sector for a My Little Derivatives Dealer set (comes with angry lynch mob and trashable Porsche), and the bottom has fallen out of the Give-a-Goat scheme. Ate the cheesecakes for lunch alone.

TANNENBAUM TANGENT: Santa was still very cool with us; not sure that we have clawed back enough lost ground yet; and he didn't go for the cheesecake routine. Are we getting stale?

AUGUST 19

Was looking at the Vegas snaps again and realized I never heard back from Ms. Leibovitz. She's so busy she probably hasn't got my messages. Perhaps I should send her a couple of the night-time shots? She'll appreciate how I've overcome some of the technical challenges. Mamma C. called to say she's on her way back. She's very excited about flying in on standard airline. Booked Mrs. D. to come in for the afternoon and give Yule Lodge a quick clean.

AUGUST 20

Mamma C. back! She brought me a striped T-shirt and a beret, and a garlic press for Poindexter. He went very pale and wouldn't touch it. Not everyone loves garlic.

THE
SERENE WAY

Poindexter's spa

AUGUST 21

Poindexter's gone off on his five day break at last. Caught him beeswaxing his desk to a high sheen just before he set off. He's doing a 100-mile motivational power walk across Montana with a bunch of Harvard alumni, then on to a detox spa on the Oregon coast, where they fast for one day, have liquids only for the next. Kris Kringle on a raft!

AUGUST 22

Momma C. still speaking French at me all the time. Me and Mrs. D. have settled back into the old routine like two spoons in a presentation box. She brought in a giant batch of marshmallow cookies, the big tea pot, and our special mugs that Poindexter thought looked too homey for a global operation like Santacorp. It was as if she'd never left. Her nephew has his own IT firm, so she got him to scan all the NoN cards. Before I'd even got through the ninth cookie, he'd created an easily searchable database complete with a fancy geomapping facility. Poindexter will be SO impressed.

AUGUST 23

Mrs. D. is doing the rounds of the workshops for a chat and some facetime with old friends, notebooks are up to date, the database works, Mamma C.'s making me an eggwhite omelette with edamame beansprouts for lunch and all's well in Santacorp. Watched the sports channel, as it is crucial to know how the season is going; team positions and popularity impact on our replica sportswear inventory. Must remember to check available dates for the October Sports Day and North Pole Baseball League play offs. I'm a Redpants man myself, but Mrs. D. always roots for the Lapland Lemmings.

AUGUST 24

78mm—starting to take shape!

Beard's now got 6 months' growth, and it's looking thick and healthy. Mamma C. thinks I should put lemon juice in the rinsewater when I wash it, to prevent yellowing. Don't know about that, but had fun with the beardputty present I got from the elves last year. Made myself some chin antlers.

AUGUST 25

Personal Training Session 7:30am

This one snuck up on me; Poindexter must have put it in without me noticing. Sarge power-walked me to the Pine Tree Testing Plantation where we spent what seemed like three days doing chin-ups on low branches. Mamma C. came down to see, and brought us some wheatgrass soda. Sarge did 245 one-handed push-ups while she was there. I am going to have to raincheck the other four birthday-gift sessions. If I carry on like this, I'll be too tired to chimney.

AUGUST 26

I hate the end of August. It's like a whole week of
Sunday evenings. The weather changes and I get all
nostalgic and antsy and weirdly creative—must be the
artist in me. Then September is my Monday morning. Had
another look at my Vegas poems. Maybe I could get them
published—under a psnowdonym, of course. Mamma C.'s in a
very jolly mood at the moment and is babbling on in French
with Poindexter. She says 'ooh là là' and 'j'adore' a lot and
they keep having 'tettatets', whatever they are. Probably
some French pastry I'm not allowed.

AUGUST 27

Poindexter came up with a crazy idea—a Santabanterblog.
Bonjour? Helloo? I can't spend my day telling everyone
what I am doing or I wouldn't get anything done. And it
would seriously eat into what little snack time I've got. I
just nod now and say: 'Hold that thought. Let's agendarize
it' and it seems to keep him quiet. I am not sure how long
I can go on working with Poindexter. Life with Mrs. D. was
so much less stressful.

Book the Grand
Arctic Salon for
the big sales
presentation in
October.

Look up 'Tettatet' in
French dictionary.

STRENGTHS AND WEAKNESSES – P

STRENGTHS:	WEAKNESSES:
Youthful	Too young
Fresh and keen	No history
Ivy league	Out of my league
Organized	Hyperactive
Doesn't know what I'm thinking	I can fool him
Techno-wizard	Techno-maniac
Hardworking	Hard work
Gets on with Mamma C.	Flirts with Mamma C.
Ambitious	Wants my job?

STRENGTHS AND WEAKNESSES – MRS. D.

Older	Set in her ways
Lots of history	Knows me too well
More synergy?	Less energy?
Makes a great cookie	Makes a great cookie
Knows what I'm thinking	Finishes my sentences
Loves Mamma C.	Tells Mamma C. all
Technophobe	Technophobe
Doesn't want my job	Should I stand on my own two feet?

SEPTEMBER 1

Didn't sleep a wink. Panic attacks are back bigtime plus night sweats and even a spot of sleepwalking, according to Mamma C. She said I got up in a daze looking for cookies around 3:00am. It's September and C-Day is on the horizon, not over the hill any more. I can almost smell it. Mamma C. says I must keep calm. I tried omm..., I tried mmm.., I tried Santa gum, but only mmm... works when I get like this. Had to resort to my Crisis Cookies. They've been up our chimney for a month, and were a bit gritty, but did the trick. Am I really up to it this year? Is it time for someone else to take on the job? But who? Poindexter seems even more anxious than me and has whittled his bonsai to a few twigs now. And I refuse to even consider Père Noël. Non, non, non.

SEPTEMBER 2

Felt better today although
a bit nauseous. Might have
an angst ulcer. Or a
hernia? Maybe both. How
will I get down a chimney
with a hernia? I would have
to parachute down and then
be airlifted out by Rudolph. I don't have time to be ill.

Talk to
Doc. Saylittle.

SEPTEMBER 3

Doc. Saylittle said ulcer and hernia were in my head. PHEW!
Left a message at Sleigh Slim to say I wouldn't be attending
classes until January next year. I need to clear the decks
so I can sort out all the purchasing, production, and people
issues. C-Day is the north,
south, east, and west of
my existence for the next
hundred days (remember to
put that in one of my poems).
Or maybe it's my 'A to Z'?
I'm so worked up I can't
even write poetry.

Plan speech.

Put others first.

SEPTEMBER 4

Poindexter arrived early to report on just-in-time status,
quality control and staff relations. He looked tired and
thin, and said the team could do with some 'motivation
and reinforcement thru' positive feedback and incentivizing
facetime.' I think maybe he meant him, too. Felt bad.
I should be thinking more about the team. Reading back

over my diary, it's all me, me, me. Am I self-obsessed now too? Called Guru O'Shaunessy but he was at a sweat lodge apparently. Time to rally the troops, so started working on a speech for the staff. Still can't find my mantra snowglobe —dipped into the cookie stash for inspiration instead.

SEPTEMBER 5

Worked on my speech with Poindexter for hours and he seems much more energized than yesterday. Ate ten cookies and felt a creative rush. Poindexter didn't think my speech needed to rhyme but I can't repress the poet in me. It's definitely coming together.

Elves, gnomes, reindeer—lend me your ~~hands~~ ears

Dasher, Dancer, Rudolph, and Prancer

Donner and Blitzen, and ^our dear Mr. Stiltskin.

Fellow citizens of the North Pole

Before us stands a daunting role.

Just three months till Christmas Day

When you send me on my sleigh.

To deliver gifts around the ~~globe~~ sphere

To good children far, and good ones near.

May they inspire us to do better

To answer each request and every ~~mute~~ letter.

To research, create, design, fulfill

These are our tasks and our joint will.

Once more in red breeches I shall go

Through the night and through the snow.

We few, ^we happy few, band of workers

United as we are in just one aim.

Hand in hand we strive together

And after Christmas Day, we start again.

SEPTEMBER 6

Looks like yesterday's speech went down quite well. Productivity figures are up, everyone seems happier than ever and a few of the elves have apparently written a song using some of my lines. TT caught wind of it and want them to go into a recording studio and make a CD. Are they serious?

SEPTEMBER 7

TT meeting 9:30am (inc. breakfast)

🎄 TEAM TANNENBAUM

. . . .

MEETING AGENDA:

SANTA SPEECH
• worldwide distribution? copyright issues

GLOBAL MARKETING STRATEGY
• fashion range concepts, branching out

Aaagh!

SEPTEMBER 9

Meeting with Tannenbaums 9:30am

Poindexter pencilled in the Tannenbaum meeting—not like him, it's normally in very definite ink. The Tannenbaums came loaded with muffins, cookies, waffles, and some full-fat, half-baked, sprinkled-with-nuts, crazy ideas.

They are skating on very thin ice. They've changed their minds about the CD—far too limited and last decade already, they said. They want my speech to be available as a remixed download—rap-style! It could be global in minutes, they screeched. And they want to put it on YouTube, secure audio, TV, handheld device and print rights, auction the film rights, and launch a range of clothing featuring some of the lines... for goodness sake.

Do people really want to walk around with my red breeches on their chest? What will they call the line? Yves Saint Nicholas or something? I didn't want my poem to be a fashion statement. It was a motivational piece, a work of art, from the heart (there I go again). It's all getting out of hand. I decided to leave the decision to Poindexter and headed for the door. I am getting to enjoy these Santrums. It brings out the actor in me and I saw fear in the Tannenbaums' eyes. I should build on that. Took a few waffles with me this time. I hate waste.

Is this a Santa I see before me?

SEPTEMBER 10

Mamma C.'s birthday this week. Having a bumpy ride with the women in my life at the moment, so I have to treat my dearest wife to a really special day. She's a Virgo, according to Poindexter, who knows all about this stuff (does the guy ever sleep?). Anyway, Virgo or no, I know exactly how to surprise her.

Bonny Vers Hair, ma chair

SEPTEMBER 12

Asked Poindexter what the latest on the Santa kittens was, and it seems they have been a real hit. It's his pet subject now and he's got them as his screensaver—they do look cute, even I have to admit it. The Ts must be like the cats that got the cream. And I suppose I've got egg on my face...

SEPTEMBER 13

Not a good day. There was a gremlin in the database. Julnisse, the elf on temporary transfer from Denmark, is up to his tricks a bit early. He usually plays his pranks in December but he's been annoying his cousins early this year. Apparently, the only way to keep him under control is to silence him with rice pudding or porridge. Mrs. D. came in specially to sort him out with her secret raisin porridge recipe. They are old friends and she used to be in charge of Elf Hazards, after all.

Clever clogs

SEPTEMBER 15

Ooh là là. Mamma C. was beyond herself. I whisked her off to Paris for dinner 'à deux' by candelight, overlooking the Eiffel Tower, and then on to the beautiful gardens and palace of Versailles. It was soooo romantic, aside from a small glitch with the SantaNav when I flew too low over the palace roof—that gold flake gets all over the place! I even tried to sing Happy Birthday in French. Mamma C. said it was just like meeting Inspector Clouseau. I know she's always been a big fan, so it was a 'triomphe' all round.

Hotel Concorde, Restaurant Astier

Hotel Concorde, 105 Rue de Pontoise, 75056 Paris

Soupe de Poissons	7.50
Omelette aux fines herbes	6.00
Magret de Canard, au confit d'orange	25.00
Filet de Boeuf aux cinq Poivres, avec salade de tomates et frites	22.00
Crème Brûlée x 2	11.00
Plat de fromages	8.00
Cabernet Sauvignon	12.99
TOTALE	92.45

Merci beaucoup

SEPTEMBER 18

California tomorrow, for the Belief Seminar. I'm trying to be open-minded about it, but I'm not looking forward to group yoga session post-lunch. I'll deliver my troop speech for the opening address and try to keep a low profile for the rest of the day. Mamma C. is coming along for the ride. She's going to shop in San Fran with the Tooth Fairy after doing her First Lady of Christmas stuff.

WEST COAST
BELIEF SEMINAR

September 19–20

Big Sur Cave & Yurt Village
Hon speaker: Mr S. N. Claus

SEPTEMBER 19

West Coast Belief Seminar

Tee shirt the Ts gave me for my slot went down well. 'Believing is not Seeing' is a great slogan and I could tell the Easter Bunny wanted one for himself. The Tooth Fairy did an excellent presentation with flowcharts and graphs on how the meaning of our existence is directly related to the existence of meaning—didn't realize she was such a brain— thought she was just into finance. Guru O'Shaunessy, turned up out of nowhere, straight from the ashram

TANNENBAUM TANGENT: Great seminar. Great location. Great weather. Great slogans. Fairytale ending. This sort of event makes being in PR worthwhile. We love our job. We love Santa. We could even learn to love Mrs D. Tried to get the Tooth Fairy to leave her agency, but she won't. Think she might be in it for the money.

with a portable sweat lodge. He had all the delegates doing 'omm...' in seconds and chanting, 'Yes, Virginia, there is a Santa Claus.' That little girl was so sweet. Despite her initial doubts, I won her round—and I still have a copy of that old editorial from the New York Sun, printed 1897, upstairs in the attic.

Dear Santa,

Just had to drop you a line to say how unreal you were at the seminar. Numero Uno. I could hardly believe my eyes. Sorry we didn't catch up at the end of your session but I had to go to work straight away. There's a lot of dental work in California, and I do kids and adults now. Let's think about doing after dinner speeches together. We could clean up.

T.F.

SEPTEMBER 23

Back to earth with a bump. Julnisse not appeased by porridge and created havoc in the factory—oat slime everywhere. He's in front of the Elfish Behavior Board tomorrow—may have to go back to Denmark.

SEPTEMBER 24

Rudolph seems a bit down in the nose so Poindexter suggested a male bonding weekend. He will research possibilities as I am JUST TOO BUSY. The California Effect is wearing off. Rudolph fancies ice fishing, if you can believe it... as if I don't spend enough time in the freezing cold! And I ain't going in no tent!

SEPTEMBER 24

Rudolph put his hoof down about the ice-fishing but I staged a convincing Santrum over camping. Rudolph can snore like you wouldn't believe, and we would have to make drafty holes in the tent for his antlers. Poindexter stepped in with a Green Friendship Program—Compromise: a low-carbon hoofprint vacation specializing in outdoor activities at the North Pole. Result. Poindexter should work at the UN. Don't tell him.

TO BRING:
- Picnic food—Mamma C.?
- Thermos
- Long johns & mitts
- Winter pjs
- Blankets & boots
- Bathing suit
- Telescope
- Camera (of course)
- Chocolate rations
- 'What a Star!' astronomy book

Mamma C. made us a great basket for the journey—homemade clam chowder (no crackers) and lo-cal organic hot chocolate for me, and a nice locally sourced grass-alfalfa sprout-and-sedge mix for Rudolph. Mrs. D.'s minnow sushi and cold worm mousse looked pretty good, too, but apparently it's for the fish. We're going to make holes in the frozen lake and spend quality time together waiting for the fish to bite. Then we'll head to the Ice n' Slice Lodge, complete with warm, sustainable log fires and outdoor solar-powered hot tub.

SEPTEMBER 25

Hole-making was exhausting—had to use emergency chocolate rations almost immediately. It was minus 150 degrees at least and I was pretty cold—even in my micro-thermal insulated suit Poindexter borrowed from NASA. I think my long johns would have been better. Rudolph was happy

Catch of the day

as a clam in his handknitted scarf from Mamma C. His antlers made perfect rods, and thanks to Mrs. D.'s bait, we caught a HUGE fish in the first hour. We spent lots of time communing with nature, contemplating our past and just chewing the fat, or grass in his case. Only downside is that—due to a rather convenient lack of opposable thumbs, Rudolph couldn't clean the fish. Guess who had to step up...

But the lodge was fabulous. Big buffet, cashmere blankets, and an extra-wide hot tub to accommodate the four-legged. We were just chilling in the bubbles, enjoying a spectacular Baked Alaska dessert (me) and a lichen lolly (Rudolph) when we were treated to the greatest show visible to the naked eye—only the Aurora Borealis! It was even better than New Year's Eve. Incredible and moving. Like nature was sending us a message. That we were just twinkles in an unfathomable galaxy. That we should appreciate our friends. That love is all there is. It was a very special moment.

Best friends forever

SEPTEMBER 26

Woke up really early and was out in the yard with my fishing poles before I remembered that I was back home. Hope Rudolph enjoyed himself. All this wilderness certainly stimulates the appetite— when I checked on him, Ol' Red was chowing down on the hay like there was no tomorrow and

WOW!!

I'd managed two bowls of cereal, double steak, and eggs and a stack of French toast before Mamma C. came down for her bio-yoghurt and wheatgerm. Apparently I still stink of fish and had to take another five showers before she let me go to the office. Showed her the Aurora Borealis shots me and R took. Think she was impressed—she was too stunned to say anything.

SEPTEMBER 27

Wish I hadn't come back. Poindexter insisted on a debriefing session—I've been gone two days and everything's suddenly color coded. He's also installed a huge glass 'Writable

Figure out how to turn off BlackBerry ring

Interface' so that we can 'co-ordinate progress, completion, and shortfall in a low impact, high-visibility matrix'. He has rigged my BlackBerry so that it goes 'ping!' and plays the opening bars of 'Here Comes Santa Claus' whenever I've got a meeting.

SEPTEMBER 28

Personal Training 7:30am

Woke up to the muffled sound of that infernal song. Found the BlackBerry in the laundry basket, with a little picture of Sarge and a flashing alert, signed Poindexter. I thought I'd cancelled those sessions, but Mamma C. gave me a look and said I certainly hadn't. I told Sarge I was still a bit achey from ice-fishing, so he rubbed me down with reindeer liniment—boy did that make my eyes burn!—and we did a five-mile power walk round the Santacorp perimeter. We followed this with ten million lunges, crunches, and stretches. Had to spend the rest of the day in the hot tub (not only can I not move, I also now stink of fish AND reindeer liniment). Don't have time for this, so put on my assertive voice and told Poindexter to reschedule the Sarge sessions until after C-Day. I don't care how many looks Mamma C. gives me.

SEPTEMBER 30

Worried about Poindexter. I don't think he ever goes home; he is always in the office when I arrive and still there when I leave. He's chained his special mug to his desk set and when I was looking in his drawer for some post-its I found a gazillion origami Christmas trees. Maybe I'll get Guru O'Shaunessy to come in for a group session. Might even put Mrs. D. on standby.

OCTOBER 1

TT popped in. They've been on a Concept Cascading Retreat and have come up with the idea of Synergy with Hallowe'en. I told them absolutely not, despite what their presentation notes say about orange and red being perfect companions. The two trays of pumpkin cupcakes went down well though.

DE

NOVEMBER

SUNDAY	MO
1	
8	
3	4
15	
10	11
22	*45 days*
17	18
29	
24	25

35 days

24	25	26	27	28	29	30
31 days						*25 days*

TANNENBAUM TANGENT: This was a red hot concept, and we would like to put on record our disappointment at the client's point blank refusal to consider the proposal. It was an inspired cross-platform synergistic festival osmosis that would have brought benefits to both sides. Some people just refuse to recognize that it's the 21st century.

OCTOBER 3

Strategy meeting and working lunch— all dept. line managers. 10:30am

'Here comes Santa Claus.' Arrgh. Still can't turn it off. Poindexter took notes at the meeting so I was free to assess panic levels. You can always gauge how things are going by looking at old Fred Pontoon in Distribution; if it's bad, his bald spot goes 40 shades of Rudolph. Pizza for lunch, choose your own toppings.

OCTOBER 4

Note from Mrs. D... The Elf Hazard Executive Board has ordered Julnisse to do five days community service with us. Do I have any suggestions? It's the North Pole Baseball World Series next week—maybe he could be on clean-up detail after the game?

OCTOBER 5

Wonder when we will get the first letter? Must find out if Stiltskin is running the sweepstake again this year. My big chocolate penny is on November 1. Took Poindexter down to the mailroom to show him how it all works. He gets very nervous away from the office but I let him keep his headset on and bring back the mailroom handbook to peruse at his desk. He was very intrigued by our elite chimney fairy unit that deals with late present requests— asked if he could tour their department. We seemed a bit short on staff down there, so I asked Poindexter to make a recruitment ad.

MAILROOM WORKFLOW:

- Three deliveries of letters daily.
- Read and copied by Wee Scanners.
- Sorted into category sacks.
- Sacks transported to Fulfilment Sheds.
- Requests are packed, barcoded, and stored by geographical region
- Toys packed into sleigh for December 24.

PLEASE NOTE: letters picked up by Santa on his round are dealt with by the elite Fast And Immediate Response Initiative Express Service (FAIRIES) trained in Last Minute Search & Deliver methods.

BE THE FASTEST

LOOK GOOD IN MIDNIGHT GREEN NEOPRENE?
Call FAIRIES toll free 0001-123-25122512 for more info

Poindexter's first draft

OCTOBER 6

Can't sleep; I have been doing this for centuries and I know that something always creeps out of the woodwork at the last minute. Remember the Great Rubik's Cube Disaster of 1981? Unbeknownst to us, the gearing arm on the sticker placement belt lost a cog, and a whole consignment came out blue—we had to write off the whole order; disappointed faces all round. Still wake up screaming about that around this time of year.

OCTOBER 7

Poindexter got unacceptably OCD about polishing his desk this morning so I have tasked him (check out my biz speak) with ticket selling for the North Pole Series. Baseball game is only a few days

- restock crisis cookie caches.
- double check the secret secret donut cubbyhole.

away, so went down to the practice nets to check out the new Redpants hitter—not bad!

OCTOBER 8

Found the mantric snowglobe! Just in time, too—I think Mamma C. has found my secret secret donut cubbyhole hidden under Rudolph's manger. She knows about the cookie caches—who else would replace them with granola bars?—but I thought I'd managed to keep the donuts under the radar.

OCTOBER 9

TT at it again. This time they want a 'deercam' to transmit direct from the sleigh on C-Day. They even drew what they think it would look like. Have these women got any sense of basic physics? Don't they realize any camera attached to the sleigh would melt during the S-space warp jumps? Anyway, all I can think about is the Redpants game tomorrow...

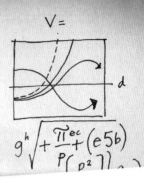

$$V =$$

$$g^h \sqrt{+ \frac{\Pi^{ec}}{P} + (e5b)}$$

TANNENBAUM TANGENT:

Okay, we were a bit hazy on Santa Space physics, but this was a very valid idea—the camera could have transmitted a historic Eve-of-Flight Live Real Time Experience before the STV took off. A perfect press moment if ever there was one.

$$+ 2 - S_u \left[\frac{2 \varepsilon_0 v_u^2}{q} \right] > B$$

OCTOBER 10

WORLD SERIES FINAL, 2:30pm
 Lapland Lemmings 5
 North Pole Redpants 4   GO REDPANTS!

What a game! Totally forgot to eat my popcorn. It was as tight as my No. 2 suit pants, but the Lemmings finally took it. They haven't won for six years, so this is great for them even though it's always hard to see my Redpants go down. Mrs. D. was beside herself. Julnisse violated the terms of his sentence by booby trapping the pitcher's mound and is now doing 14 days hard labor in the candy cane refinery.

OCTOBER 11

Poindexter took a swig of my hot double-double chocolate with vanilla whip cream by mistake, and went into full-on sugar rush. He went very pale, and started shaking. We had to medicate him with miso soup via a dropper and get him to bite down on a spelt and alfalfa seed bar, which seemed to do the trick. Put him in the recovery position—he didn't recall a thing when he came round.

Recovery position

1. Check for any injuries. If the person is hurt, don't move him or her! Call 911 and ask for an ambulance.
2. Bend arm to stop person rolling over.
3. Gently roll person onto side.
4. Bend leg to support position.
5. Tilt head back and tuck hand under chin to keep mouth open.
6. Make sure someone is keeping an eye on him or her.

OCTOBER 12

TT have retroscheduled the monthly meet from 15th to today. Had to take time out from the Temporary Mail Room Operative interviews. If I'm not there to slam on the brakes those women will run riot, and Poindexter seems to think all their ideas are great. Apparently the Ts are going to a 'Book Fair' in Germany. Told them to keep an eye out for D.E.R. Weihnachtsmann—he heads up the German franchise and is very knowledgeable. He's actually been around longer than me! They

Here's a picture of old Dieter from 1849, pre-merger. Great guy, but always makes me feel a bit of a lightweight, intellectually speaking.

said they are going to try and capitalize on the Santa kitten campaign, open up a whole new media forum for the Santa brand, and initiate a bidding war for the rights to my memoirs and the 'Santa rap' CD. Completely forgot about my memoirs! Told them I hadn't even started and they said not to worry—nobody writes their own—and that they'd just get in a couple of hacks to ghostwrite it and I just sign it. I told them no way—who could possibly impersonate my particular writing style?

OCTOBER 14

Finally in—Action Dossier from the Belief Seminar (don't rush yourselves guys). News is bad. Figures indicate we are hemorrhaging belief marketshare this year, especially to the self-help industry who encourage belief in yourself rather than anything else. Depressing. Credibility Index shows figures on the rise this month, but adjust this for seasonal factors (belief seems to be lowest in June—the public is so fickle) and the underlying slow downturn is apparent. Maybe I should pay a bit more attention to the Ts after all.

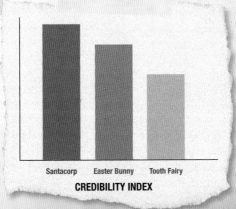

Santacorp   Easter Bunny   Tooth Fairy

CREDIBILITY INDEX

Tore this out of the Action Dossier. Wish I hadn't.

OCTOBER 16

Took ages to get to sleep, and then had
my nightmare, the one where I'm melting,
getting smaller and smaller and end up
shouting inside a glass tree ornament and
no-one can see or hear me. Woke up and
polished off the sack of candies Mamma C. is hoarding
for the trick or treaters, then had a clementine out of
the healthy options sack to balance out the bad sugars,
so that's not so bad.

OCTOBER 17

Called Guru O'Shaunessy for a pick-me-up session.
Om-baubling not enough and the mantric snowglobe just
makes me feel snowed under and all alone with the deer
in a glass bubble. Guru O'S gave me a new affirmation and
suggested I get out my 12 worry beads of Christmas
from last year. I had forgotten about them, but I'll start
to carry them in my pocket again for instant access.

AFFIRMATION 5:
If I don't believe in
myself, why should
anybody else?

Each bead = Happy thought

OCTOBER 18

Sent Poindexter with a team out to monitor the nationwide grotto roll-out. Random spot checks—grotto hygiene, height, width, twinkle factor, the usual—keep the store managers on their toes. And it helps us choose for 'Best Kept Grotto' at the end of the year.

Grotto fabulous! Love the giant star!

BEST KEPT GROTTO 1999

OCTOBER 20

8:00pm Santacorp Gala, GRAND Arctic Salon

It's crunchtime; every department CEO has to step up to the plate and show what they've been doing all year. Had a bit of a snooze when accounts or logistics were droning on— I can only take so many flow charts and Venn diagrams. But it was good to see what the creatives have up their sleeves: toy classics with a twist, cult imports, niche items and smart repackaging of the Cabbage Patch Doll, if you can believe it. Best bit was the Emergency Services' simulated disaster demo; spontaneous combustion in the Cuddly Cow stuffed animal, due to an explosive reaction of GM fake fur to organic kapok fabric in the presence of cellulose. Button-eye shrapnel all round. What a show! Felt cheered, I've got a great team, we're gonna make it a C-Day to remember.

OCTOBER 21

Temporary Mailroom
Operatives all signed up;
Mamma C.'s already got them
repainting the old bunkhouses
they'll live in when the
letters start coming. The
FAIRIES unit has gone off
to an undisclosed location for
special ops refresher course
and endurance exercises.

COFFEE   LAVENDER

EMERALD   SALMON

*what do you
think of these?*

OCTOBER 22

Santa Seminar

This is where I show our Santa Trainees how to run their
grottos, and how to be me. Good to see old familiar faces
(we recruit heavily from Hollywood) and plenty of young ones
with campus indie beards. Most of the grunt training is done
by experienced impersonators but I give a keynote speech to
get people in the mood, along with a personal demo of the
Santacorp Way to 'Ho Ho Ho' (no-one is ever quite as jolly
as me...). Got a standing ovation
this year! At the end of the
day the trainees pick up their
uniforms, customized beards, a
goody bag with a multipack of
candy canes, Santa Gum, and a
signed photo of Rudolph. This
year, courtesy of TT, they
also got my Santa 'rap' CD
and some motivational flashcards
to boost morale during slack
periods, along with a Santa
kitten keychain.

OCTOBER 23

We still haven't figured
out what will be this
year's Top Toy... It will
be too late soon. Still
think about that awful
trip to the Missed the
Boat warehouse, an
abandoned facility in
Minnesota where we
store all the My Little Ponies, Buzz Lightyears etc. that
came in too late to satisfy demand; nothing sadder than a
must-have toy that doesn't arrive until C-Day +1.

Conference call
with Père Noël +
Sinterklaas—make
sure Continental
grotto operations
are going smoothly.

OCTOBER 24

Serious bearding now. Very patriarchal. Poindexter took a
picture and Photoshopped it to show what the beard will
look like in December—and it's right on track! Now
we can send the photo off to the Santa Trainees.
Their beards have to look as much like mine as
possible to avoid disappointment.

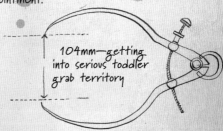

104mm—getting
into serious toddler
grab territory

OCTOBER 25

News from TT; they have definite interest on the memoirs
and the CD, and sure-fire Finnish sale. They say they need
presentation material, and got very snippy when I said that I
wouldn't be able to do anything until December 26.

OCTOBER 26

Woke up with a great idea. Maybe my memoirs could include some of my best photographs. Rushed out to take close-ups of freshly fallen snowflakes and capture their symmetrical but unique beauty, then rushed back inside to write it. Wrote this instead—this memoir business is harder than it sounds.

A crystal clear winner!

OCTOBER 27

Put in a call to Annie L. to tell her that I was likely to become a published author and photographer in the not-too-distant future. Didn't want her to miss out. Weird that she never gets back to me. Oh well, she had her chance. Wonder how the deal is going for my memoirs? I really have to get writing—can't have someone ghostwriting or they'll be sure to put in all sorts of embarrassing stuff. Santa's got a reputation to live up to, after all. Can't have all this 'bunions-and-all' writing that seems to be making the rounds.

I DID IT— MY SLEIGH

OCTOBER 31

Poindexter's out of town for the weekend with The Hallowe'en Group. He didn't even take his BlackBerry so it sounds like an in-camera session with his fellow Hallowe'eners at an undisclosed location—they always take this day very seriously and I have to admit, he was being very cloak and dagger. He was wearing his dark black suit and wouldn't even let me give him a lift—said he could arrange his own transport this time. He was here one minute and gone the next. Strange. Poor guy—I'm glad he's taking some time out before the big rush. He's been looking so stressed recently. His OCD has finally stretched beyond the realms of his desk space, and now takes in the entire office. He has even bought me my own personalized desk set. Like I would know what to do with one of those—so far, I keep my licorice sticks in it. Some quality time with Hallowe'en Group relatives will do Poindexter a whole lot of good.

Find number for Annie L.'s agent.

What do I need with this?

NOVEMBER 1

Woke up at 3:00am with my old friend Mr. Angst, after dreaming I was buried alive under a mountain of Cabbage Patch dolls. Whoever said 'November is the cruellest month' was right. I have just that extra bit more time to think, which I don't have AT ALL in December, so I worry about all the things that could go wrong. It's weird, but I actually miss Poindexter and his strategic thinking for once. He calms me down when he is not trying to tidy me up. Went to the factory to see how they were getting on with rebuilding my reinforced multi-tiered letter intray—it toppled under the weight last year and broke. It's still not ready. Went to the Fulfilment Shed to check if the new barcode machine had arrived from Seattle. No sign of it—might have to rely on a simple stamp if all else fails. Checked phone messages. Nothing from Poindexter, nothing from Annie L., no news from TT even. Seems like it's No-no-November.

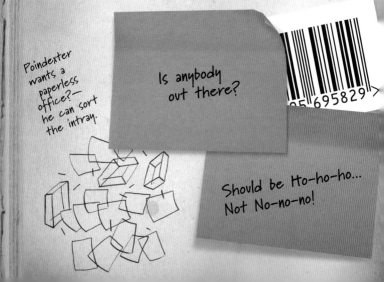

Poindexter wants a paperless office?— he can sort the intray.

Is anybody out there?

05 695829

Should be Ho-ho-ho... Not No-no-no!

NOVEMBER 2

Dreamt Poindexter had been poached by Easter Bunny Inc. and was given huge bucks to write a kiss 'n' tell about me. Woke up at 5:00am and didn't want to disturb Mamma C., so went straight round to Mrs. D. for some hot cocoa with whipped cream, ice cream and dunkin' marshmallows. I had to ring the bell four or five times before she heard me, but it was worth the wait. Fortunately, Mr. D. is allergic to marshmallows, so it was only polite to have a refill. Took the recipe home. I feel a chocolate month coming on.

MRS. D'S HOT 'N' COLD COCOA RECIPE

INGREDIENTS:
1. Generous handful of chocolate chips (70 percent cocoa)
2. Scant cup of milk (low fat works almost as well)
3. Generous dollop of ice cream
4. Ditto double whipped cream
5. Delicate cinnamon snowflake (optional)
6. Generous handful of marshmallows

METHOD:
Combine 1 and 2. Heat.
Sink 3.
Float 4 Quite a treat.
Sprinkle 5. Be Neat.
Dunk 6. Eat.

Think positively.
What else can
go wrong?

HEALTH WARNING:
FOR SANTA'S CONSUMPTION ONLY.
NEVER TO BE SERVED TO
POINDEXTER OR MR. D.

NOVEMBER 5

What the Holly & Ivy? A limo arrived at the factory at 8:00am this morning flanked by security vehicles. A guy dressed in a very sharp suit spoke to Stiltskin and asked if he could direct him to my place to deliver an envelope marked 'Priority.' Mr. S. refused and made the guy leave it with him, along with the biggest box of chocolates either of us has ever seen. He brought both over to Yule Lodge. At first I thought it might be an exhausted Poindexter's resignation letter, but jingle my angsty bells, it was the first 'Dear Santa' letter of the year. From a celebrity child with satellite surveillance capacity. Bribing Santa. Bad move. Chocolates looked delicious tho'.

Dear Santa

I think you should know that I have been better than good this year. I have been perfect. I am well-behaved, kind, considerate, thoughtful, and very unspoilt for a celebrity prodigy. I am top of my class and when I am out shopping on Fifth Avenue with my friends I even help old ladies cross the street. My parents describe me as an A-plus child in an A-list world. I am getting a nose job from them for Christmas.

I have most things money can buy, as you can imagine, but one thing I don't have and which would make the other girls like sooo jealous is a unicorn. I realize it might be difficult to get one down the chimney. Please put him in the fourth stable from the left at the end of the drive. I will leave a map for you.

I would like an absolutely pure white unicorn with no markings and the horn must be real silver, not just plated. I suggest you let me know well in advance when you plan to deliver the unicorn so that I can warn the security guards.

Don't park on the lawns or wake my parents.

Many thanks

Chuck the chocolates.

File letter under Z plus.

NOVEMBER 6

Yesterday's letter got me thinking about some of the great ones I've received over the years. They are all archived chronologically and kept in the Letter Library. Mrs. D. is still in charge of filing and dusting. I rang her to ask which one was her favorite and we both agreed that the letter from little Abe Lincoln was one of the best. She got it out of the library so we could reminisce over another hot 'n' cold cocoa—I hear chocolate is very good for serotonin levels and I do feel better after drinking a good slurp. And then I go all hot and cold, which I suppose means it is working.

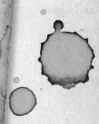

Dear Santa

I try my best to be good, fair, and true. I hope I have managed to be all three this year. In the hope that you agree and once you have delivered gifts to all the other well-behaved and deserving children of the world I would truly appreciate an axe and a copy of 'Common Sense' by Tom Paine.

with regards
Abraham Lincoln, aged 10

An historic letter—still brings tears to my eyes.

NOVEMBER 7

Where's Poindexter? I thought he said he was going away
for the weekend. It's been a week. No calls, no messages,
nothing. Called Guru O'Shaunessy but got his voicemail. It
just said 'Ommmm...' Not even 'Leave a message'. Have they
set up a rival company? The Ts haven't even heard from
him. Can't sleep. Can't concentrate.
Can't delegate. Worst of all, I can't
stop eating. I cleared the refrigerator
at midnight. Everything in it. Gone.
Like locusts had arrived with one of
our deliveries. Mamma C. did not fall
for that. There's a padlock on it now.

Get elves to
break padlock.

Must stop eating.
Try to put the
'om' back in
comfort food.

NOVEMBER 8

Poindexter's back. He'd scheduled his week away on my
BlackBerry instead of my calendar—like I know how to
access that. I was soo relieved to see him I couldn't even
pretend to be angry. He's like a new man. Relaxed,
rejuvenated. There's something different about him but I can't
put my finger on it. It's like he has just had the best sleep
of his life. Refrigerator still locked. What happened to
trust? She said it went the same way her cupcakes did.

SLEIGH **SLIM**
North Pole

Just checking you are doing okay, Mr. Claus. We realize you are now entering your busiest period, and we wish you all the best in your mission. In our experience, stress can lead to serial comfort eating and we have devised coping strategies for just this eventuality. We've included a handy leaflet for your reading pleasure.

Yours truly,
Dorothy

NOVEMBER 9

Poindexter was like a whirlwind today. He'd done his 'To do' list before dawn, sorting glitches in the database, gremlins in the production line, and glumness in the elf camp. The guy's inhuman. He had even tidied my desk by the time I got to it—said my licorice sticks had infected the pens. I was just on my way to the canteen for an emergency breakfast meeting when I was forced by Mamma C. to listen to the talking scales yell 'One at a time, please.' I need confirmation of my worth, not my body weight.

FEELING FESTIVELY FRAZZLED?

SEE THE CARROTS FOR THE COOKIES!

COMFORT DOESN'T = FOOD

... see inside for coping strategies to help you

NOVEMBER 10

Thanks to Poindexter, I managed to find some really useful things on my desk, including my S-box designs I'd forgotten about. Patents still hasn't got back on that one. No answer when I called.

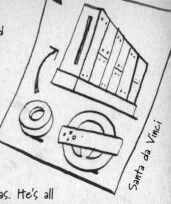

Santa da Vinci

NOVEMBER 16

E-mail arrived from Sinterklaas. He's all BlackBerry'd up too. He said the steamboat trip from Spain to Holland was unreal, as usual, and that riding over the rooftops on his white horse gave him a real kick. He says I should go with him next year. I can't see myself in the saddle somehow. Rudolph agreed. In fact, he thought it was a seriously bad idea. He's always so worried about my welfare. Apparently the Dutch children leave a shoe near the hearth and a carrot for Sinterklaas's horse. His knights do the chimney work and exchange the carrot for candy. How easy is that? He gets to wear a pretty stylish outfit and his beard is so much tidier than mine. Sometimes I think I might have job envy. But then I remember I'm allergic to tulip pollen.

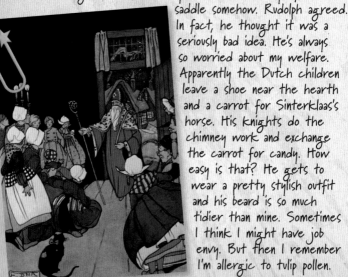

Wonder who Sinterklaas's life coach is?

Ask Mrs. D. about a new soundproof cushion cover.

Call me after my birthday on December 6. I'll teach you to ride.

NOVEMBER 18

OMG. OMG. OMG. Just over a month to C-Day! Woke up at 3:00am with a serious case of the nerves... a full-blown panic attack. Poor Mamma C. was snoring beside me and I reached for my soundproof Screaming Cushion so she wouldn't wake up. But where did all the holes come from? Apparently, moths like screaming cushions, too... Breathed deeply and tried to quietly Ommm... bauble it all away. Even that didn't work so grabbed the spare cookie under the mattress. That didn't work. Rang Guru O'Shaunessy. Got his voicemail. I didn't want to worry anyone. I wanted to do it Munch style. No sound effects. So I did the only thing possible. I ordered a takeout pizza and gave the code so that they'd deliver to the back door. I ate it outside in my pajamas and slippers—just like when I used to have to smoke my pipe in the snow before I gave up. Mamma C. found me—said she looked out the window and saw a trail of steam. I'll have to start ordering thin crust. Now she is threatening to install a pizza alarm at the back door. This is no life.

NOVEMBER 24

Feeling much better. Thanksgiving is THE BEST day.
I love everything about it—except possibly the sharing bit.
Mamma C. took the padlock off the refrigerator for the
day—I persuaded her it didn't seem right on a day when we
were giving thanks for it. What is it about turkey? I can't
get enough of the stuff. Must be the L-tryptophan—I always
sleep like a baby afterwards—sometimes even at the table!
The Lemmings thrashed the Redpants in a charity game
in the morning. All the money raised goes to the Retired
Elves Foundation (REF). Rudolph took mascot duties too
far and tried to do some deerleading, too. Now he's got
serious neckache. Something else to worry about.

We invited Mr. and Mrs. D. and Babbo Natale over from Italy
to join us this year. He arrived with delicious food—panettone,
Parmesan and mozzarella cheese, and a mountain of scrumptious
mascarpone. Poindexter was working at the soup kitchen

so he couldn't come. Mamma C.
took loads of photos—not sure
that we needed quite so many
of old Babbo. He's a bit too
smooth for my liking and ate
like a bird. He left me a
DVD of a movie called 'Blow
Out' and his tailor's business
card—not sure why. He
knows I've got my own suits.

What's so cool about him?

DI MAGGIO
ESCLUSIVO

MILANO · ROMA · FIRENZE

NOVEMBER 25

Felt like a goose stuffed for Christmas this morning, but Mamma C. was too busy learning how to make fresh pasta with Babbo Natale to give me one of her looks. Phew. She wants to learn Italian now. It's all 'Chow this' and 'Chow that.' I thought I was meant to be on a diet. She talks more nonsense than the talking scales sometimes. Maybe they'll be learning Italian next.

Schedule physical for Rudolph.

Go cold turkey. No more sandwiches!

NOVEMBER 26

Thanksgiving's done and it's panic time. Nothing between us and C-Day! Everyone is very keyed up, especially Poindexter. I think he's overspraying his bonsai plant. Trying to keep calm because it doesn't make sense to go off too early and burn out. Do we have time for a team-building day with Guru O'S? Got the elves to work on a duplicate set of worry beads.

Did I commission focus group? When? Check with Poindexter.

WHERE IS LIST OF LISTS!!!!!!

Book Guru O'S in for a group session asap?

Do bonsais get too tense?

NOVEMBER 27

TT sent in the results of their Gift Set Focus Group. What do we pay them for? It's far too late to be of any use, but it did confirm my gut feeling—that nobody really likes a gift set—it's like the giver hasn't put any love or thought into it. Yet it continues to do well over in the Corporate Rewards section... go figure.

NOVEMBER 28

Rudolph's birthday on December 1; think it's a big one—maybe that's why he's been such a gloom-bucket this year. Book Little Arctic Salon and the Hay Yard for dancing. What can you get a deer who has everything?

Will one be enough?

NOVEMBER 30

Mrs. D. brought in my new Screaming Cushion cover—and she's outdone herself this time—now it's not only soundproof but waterproof! Showed Poindexter how it works but I don't think he was impressed. He said he'd stick with his bonsai and began to vigorously rake the gravel garden that surrounds it. Whatever works, I suppose...

Nice work, Mrs. D.!

PRESENT IDEAS
FOR RUDOLPH:

- antler muffs
- muzzle balm
- gourmet granola

- hoof varnish
  [or hoof spa]

DECEMBER 1

RUDOLPH'S BIRTHDAY

Jingaling! Great party. Rudolph shy
at first, but after a couple of hot
mushroom shakes he started dancing
the Macarena—hope I don't have
to book another physical for him.
A stormin' performance of Rockin' Robin
won him the Karaoke Competition, hooves
down. Mamma C. gave him a magnum of Marshmallow and
Mistletoe Nose Balm, I gave him a framed photograph
of us at the fishing hole so he can hang it up in his stable,
Poindexter presented him with a Leatherman™ Antler File,
and the rest of the sleigh team clubbed together and
bought him a Weekend Dog Sledding Experience so he can
see what it's like on the other side. Fabulous grass, sedge,
and lichen layer cake with red and white frosting. It ended
with us all singing a version of Rudolph's very own song.
Poindexter advised me not to write down the words as
they are copyright, but everybody knows the one I mean.

DECEMBER 2

Should have started Brandy Practice yesterday but completely
forgot! I wish some habits would fade away—I'm perfectly
happy to take the cookies and milk everyone
leaves, but why do some people still cling on
to that old 'brandy by the chimney' thing?
My intolerance seems to keep getting
worse each year and I've had to double the
homeopathic dose this time. It's the only
way to build up resistance for the big day.
Took two slugs to make up for yesterday.

1 2 3 4 5 6 7 8 9 10 11 12 13 14

Rock on

DECEMBER 3

Preliminary report in from the Wee Scanners team; early letters show no distinct trend in requests; let's hope it stays that way.

DECEMBER 5

Annoyingly cheery postcard of Amsterdam in from Sinterklaas, telling us how well it all went, and how much everyone loved him, and that the favorite toy in Holland this year was SuperMario Windmill Edition. Now he's off to his Turkish hideaway for the next six months, lucky guy.

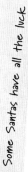

Some Santas have all the luck

ATTN S. CLAUS:

Wee Scanner McNulty here with news of toy trends vis à vis children's letters. So far, we have the usual requests for dolls, toy cars, and ponies. And of course, there's always one who wants a swimming pool... (we went with the second choice toy—a talking robot dog). But overall, no spikes in demand for anything particular yet. So far, so good!

DECEMBER 6

The pixies in the Remote Control Model Vehicle Inspection Pits have gone on strike! They want shorter hours, a revised dining hall menu and a crèche! I suspect it was Julnisse's Last Stand. He was sent back to Denmark, but has obviously left a sleeper cell. At least the brandy's tasting better.

DECEMBER 8

Must hand it to TT, they go down fighting. They are still going on about how the sack is so 'brand contra;' they have finally realized that a manbag is far too small, but now they think that we should go instead with a selection of different sized cute gift boxes in the signature Santa red and white, and a 'With love from Santa' sticker. In a heart shape. How am I supposed to juggle a bunch of giftboxes and go down a chimney? And heart shapes? I may throw up.

TANNENBAUM TANGENT: The client has no conception of brand reinforcement via ambient accessorizing. It is very frustrating as this is our specialist field. Poindexter explained about Sack Space, but there seems no reason why it could not work with our gorgeous gift boxes. Our contract is up on December 24, and let us tell you, we are not comfortable about renewing it.

10 11 12 13 15

DECEMBER 9

Poindexter has covered the Writable Interface with circles and arrows that he says show the dynamic flow of the Santasystem and the rate at which 'potential' collapses into 'outcome.' Me and Mrs. D. are sticking to the notebooks and ticking things off when they're done—I brought her in for the final push to C-Day. I hope Poindexter isn't too upset. She brought him a hot chocolate this morning, but he said he'd stick with his skinny latte. Of course, I had to drink it.

Call Pixie Mediation Services ASAP.

Need more notebooks and sticky notes.

Where are the worry beads?

DECEMBER 10

Poindexter negotiated a settlement at the inspection pits—managed to avert a crisis by bringing in the Pixie Mediation Services (PMS). We are going with a new menu, and the crèche will be put into the Planning Schedule as soon as any of them have children.

16 17 18 19 20 21 22 23 24 25

DECEMBER 11

No time for a Team Building day now, so Mamma C. suggested we had a Motivational Movie evening instead. Closed the workshops early, and Poindexter shipped in a big screen television and a freezer truck full of Santicles—the cinnamon and lichen flavors always seem to go down well. We watched Elf, and Miracle on 34th Street (the 1947 classic original, of course) followed by gingersnaps and mulled blackberry punch. (Bad Santa was screened later—it upsets some of the elves.) It was a great idea, really got us all into the mood and ready for the big day.

Check in on the deer.

Chase Wee Scanners for toy update! This is urgentissimo.

DECEMBER 12

Half way there! Twelve sleeps to go. I feel like a partridge in a pear tree while visions of sugar plums dance round my head! So much to do I can't even think straight. Poindexter organized a Sitrep Shower (department heads report in to me at ten-minute intervals and tell it like it is). Eek.

1 2 3 4 5 6 7 8 9 10 11 12 13 1

SANTACORP DIVISION	MY NOTES
1. Cuddly Toys	fluffy sharks?
2. Books and Print	what's with all this mango stuff?
3. Games and Puzzles (non-electronic)	tried to monopolize me (ho, ho, ho)
4. Baby Toys	there's such a thing as too cute
5. Dolls and Action Figures	why haven't they got one of me?
6. Paints and Crayons	'blood'-filled vampire pens—not so sure
7. Electronic Games and Consoles	they didn't even mention my S-box
8. Activity Toys	re-purpose last year's surplus fooballs?
9. Movie and TV Tie-ins	contractual small print—over to P!
10. Model Toys	check new glue reg. compliance
11. Bicycle, Scooters and Skates	just a bit too active for me
12. Novelty toys and One-offs	haven't turbo tortoises been done already?

DECEMBER 13

Arrgh!

DECEMBER 15

TT's last meeting; they weren't at all in the seasonal spirit. Didn't even bring cupcakes. Apparently the Santa Wrap is now all over the Internet, which is great, but everyone is downloading it for free, and they can't control it. Could not help but snigger into my beard. Poindexter has it on his MP3 (whatever that is).

TO: SANTA
FROM: REQUISITION DEPT

We have been advised that a consignment of kapok fabric has been impounded at the Canadian border and will not get to us until after 12/25. Can get locally sourced but will bust budget. Shall we go for it?

Test run the NoN database—use Mother Theresa and Adolf Hitler templates.

3 16 17 18 19 20 21 22 23 24 25

DECEMBER 16

Poindexter has actually suggested we do Secret Santa. Hello? What is the matter with the man? Where does he think he works? Made it clear that all Secret Santas are non-unionized scabs—we have no jurisdiction over them, and they seem to just throw away the rulebook when it comes to C-Day. The quality of presents I've seen from them is appalling. If Earthsiders want to give each other presents, I just wish they'd use a different name! Forced to eat six blackbottom cupcakes I'd brought in for the office, just to calm down enough and get on with list checking.

DECEMBER 17

Test ran suit No. 1 suit and split the pants. OMG! Got Mrs. D. to mend them—maybe she can put a bit of extra material in. Mamma C. will go seriously mad if she finds out. I've got no choice now—will have to do three days on the Yule Be Leaner Miracle Shake 'n' Soup program. The shakes taste like cold gritty wallpaper paste and the soups taste like hot gritty wallpaper paste, but whaddaya gonna do?

Order another crate of heartburn syrup—cinnamon flavor.

Must be the wrong pants?

1 2 3 4 5 6 7 8 9 10 11 12 13 14

DECEMBER 18

Abandoned shake diet. Did my surprise
workshop tour. I don't tell them when
I am coming because I don't want them
to de-focus or waste time tidying it up
for me. Hung around in the Paint & Varnish
shop and they let me finish off a couple
of rocking horses. Very relaxing.

one of mine!

FORGOT TO SAY: The Tannenbaums
turned up for a working lunch—not the best timing—but
they bought goodie bags for everyone so I stuck around.
Thinking about it, maybe they have a point, and we should
up the Santa profile. We brainstormed for a bit; Flakes of
Snow could be out soon, as well as the Santa 'rap' CD, but
I confessed that the memoirs weren't so easy to write.
Then I had a lightbulb moment. Maybe they could publish
this diary? Of course, some bits—especially the cookie
bits and the exercise bits and the Mamma C. sending
me to the stable bits—would need some
slight editing, I'd be first to admit, and
they would have to get it approved by
Legal, but it's a start, no?

DECEMBER 19

Mamma C. and me had our annual quiet
time, pre-rush intimate dinner for two.
She made me my favorite meatloaf
with hash browns, and peach cobbler
to follow. Felt better immediately.

3 16 17 18 19 20 21 22 23 24 25

DECEMBER 20

Dasher and Vixen have
athlete's hoof...

DECEMBER 21

Wee Scanners report no
letters in for 24 hours;
is there a problem
Earthside?

Call Doc. Saylittle

Dip hooves in
cinnamon and
ginger paste and
rub down with
orange peel

Dr Saylittle

URGENT MESSAGE
TO: SANTA
FROM: DOLLS

Production Line 6b reports
that entire batch of GI
Joes came through with
only one eye. Advise?

Test run Santanav
again and double-
check Disambiguation
Drive.

DECEMBER 22

NoN database up and running;
have Mrs. D. on discreet
standby with back-up.

Don't forget spare
underwear, and
Nut & Raisin No-Fat
Crunchy Balls
in snack sack.

Mission briefing
with FAIRIES
2:00pm

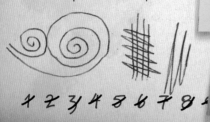

DECEMBER 23

Last beard inspection before C-Day; looking good but a bit short, so Mamma C. wove in some extensions for the Full Santa effect, in case I am glimpsed. Don't like to disappoint!

Poindexter has set up a huge chartroom, plotted me a lowest-possible-energy itinerary using geostationary satellites, and switched all communication devices to the same frequency. He looked so happy and fulfilled. Did not have the heart to tell him he won't be able to contact me (something to do with timeshifts bending radio frequency) and anyway, me and the deer (and the STV) know this route with our eyes closed. And frequently do it that way.

3 ~~16~~ ~~17~~ 18 ~~19~~ ~~20~~

FROM: STUFF YOU INC.	
TO: supplying 1,000 tons high grade kapok @ $15,000 per ton	
Sub total	$150,000.00
Discount for bulk buy @ 10%	$15,000.00
Sub total	$135,000.00
Rush fee	$2,700.00
TOTAL	$137,700.00
TERMS: 28 DAYS	

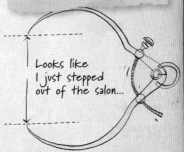

Looks like I just stepped out of the salon...

Switch no. 3 Barbie™ production line to GI Joe mode to make up shortfall. (Note: recycle one-eyed Joes as Pirate Joe?)

CHRISTMAS EVE

SUNSET

This is it! Just about to do my last rounds to make sure all is sleigh-shaped, hunky dory, and ready to roll. Poindexter showed me how to access

CHECKLIST

* Co-ordinate weather reports and feed in Santanav (POINDEXTER)
* Spot check delivery manifest to make sure it marries up with itinerary (Poindexter)
* Make sure I have the Naughty or Nice notebook with Mrs. D.'s list in for backup (ME)
* Hot mashed potato with ginger and cranberries for the reindeer (ME)
* Stash snack sack and secret snack sack in STV (ME)
* Remember 2007! Do not take off without FAIRIES liaison officer (ME)
* Gas up STV and grease runners (MAINTENANCE)
* Soot goggles! (ME)
* Check deer harnesses and antlers for hidden cameras; don't trust TT (ME)

the manifest/itinerary on my BlackBerry. Then he had to blow into a paper bag until his panic attack passed.

8.00PM

Workshops all silent, everyone standing by their lathes. Warehousing on target, everything arranged in order of delivery, and the conveyor belts oiled up. Maintenance running last checks on bits of the STV I didn't know it had. Poindexter using up another paper bag.

9.00PM

Went off into my quiet corner for a few ohm-baubles and some serious work with the worry beads. Mrs. D. brought me a mug of hot chocolate and six of her special marshmallow cookies, but I could only manage one.

10.30PM

Signed off everybody's worksheet. Mamma C. brushed me down with a de-linter and Mrs. D. repolished my hat bell. Called Père Noël to wish him good luck. Told security not to admit the Tannenbaums under any circumstances—I refuse to be on live cable feed or whatever they seem to want.

11.30PM

Watching STV being loaded, the deer hitched on. If I am gonna drive it, I want to know what it's packing. Rudolph looks so full of va va voom—hope there wasn't too much ginger in his hot bran. I can see that Liaison Officer Le Fay—our special last-minute FAIRIES operative—is strapped in at the back, ready to rush late present requests back through Sack Space; it is his first tour, and he is muttering 'hut hut hut' to himself—I think it's a kind of mantra.

Oh, it all takes me back to that first leap up into the midnight sky, the bells jingling, the freezing air scorching my cheeks, the ice crystals forming in the beard... Nearly time to go. Kiss from Mamma C...

Good luck everybody!

A FINAL NOTE

Yesterday all my Christmases came at once. Hot tub, hot lunch, hotparty, and hot prospect—sounds like the Tannenbaums are going to go ahead and publish my diary! Lets me off the hook with writing any memoirs...

This morning I was having a lovely dream about being in the warm and bubbly with Rudolph, chewing the choc, when I woke up to find a huge batlike shape looming over me. Melt my muffins in the microwave, it was only Poindexter! That guy doesn't relax even after the biggest 48 hours in the universe. He was projecting charts, graphs, and one of those cake diagrams (which of course made me hungry) onto the walls of my bedroom, casting all kinds of shadows. Do pajamas and PowerPoint presentations really go together? There I was thinking I was in trouble for my inflight snack consumption but the diagram shows market share apparently. We can't have our cake and eat it, according to Poindexter, and we need to work out how to improve systems, flow, and delivery for next year ALREADY.

The party's over, it's C-Day plus 1, or Boxing Day to Earthsiders in the UK. He suggested we draw up two Action Plans—one for each of us to implement. I tried to put it off for a while but he said there is no time like the present. I said I'd barely had time to open my presents! He gave me a look.

AXIMIZING C-DAY PERFORMANCE:
CTION BY POINDEXTER

. Resolve friction burn issue. Offer 100-Yule-Token reward for inventing eco-friendly lubricant?
. Activate newly trademarked Tannenbaum Trend Unit Monitoring Service (TANTRUMS) for next year.
. Overcome new housing challenges, including solar panels, turf roofs, and wind turbines, to avoid delays and damage.
. Upgrade NoN program with a new category—mostly nice, only sometimes naughty? To account for 10 percent increase in 'naughties' this year.
. Instigate regular team talks.

What? More team talks?

ACTION BY SANTA

1. Keep sleigh load at current levels or below—no more ponies!
2. Keep listening to the talking scales and Mamma C.'s nutritional advice.
3. Continue with successful 'No toy of the year' strategy.
4. Invite Annie L. to lunch.
5. Suggest Julnisse does internship with Père Noël this time.
6. Keep team happy.*

I liked point 6 best and came up
with new lines for my poem:
But when our work is done, and all gifts given
Brief respite and then we must be driven
To do good, to do better, to do our best
On Santa's laurels we cannot rest.

Dear Santa

I thought you might appreciate some feedback on your delivery—my Mom is always saying how important that is, and I want to be rich and famous like her.

First of all, you did not warn us what time you would arrive like I asked you to, so that was not a good start.

Second of all, there were some marks on the grass and my dad was pretty cross about those, and I know I did not make them when I last tested my Porsche in the driveway.

Third of all, and most importantly, I was very disappointed not to get the unicorn. I specifically requested it, and not getting it ruined my Christmas. Do you know what it is like not to get what you want? You can't just let kids down. It's just not fair. My dad says I could sue for emotional damage, and I heard him talking to his lawyer at the restaurant last night. Sam Jr. III mentioned something about a reality check so you will probably be getting some information on how much to make it out for.

And what was with the book you left? Never heard of 'Little Women.' Is it going to be made into a film or something? Maybe I could do an audition.

Anyways, I hope this has been helpful. I will write you again in October and I hope you deliver the unicorn this time. You really need to up your game, Santa.

best wishes